# HIGH PHE

IN

# THEORY AND PRACTICE

BY

SIR RALPH F.-PAYNE-GALLWEY, Bart.

LONGMANS, GREEN, AND CO.
39 PATERNOSTER ROW, LONDON
NEW YORK, BOMBAY, AND CALCUTTA
1913

# CONTENTS

## CHAPTER VI

## CHAPTER VII

# HIGH PHEASANTS:

## IN THEORY AND PRACTICE

### CHAPTER I

*The targets, and how they were arranged—The effect of wind on a charge of shot—Why a gun shoots a little high at horizontal birds, and a little low at birds overhead.*

IN this treatise I propose to describe the experiments I have lately made to test the capabilities of a gun on pheasants at different elevations, as well as to treat generally on the shooting of high pheasants.

I will commence with the theoretical aspect of the subject, as exemplified in perpendicular versus horizontal target practice. Of course, horizontal shooting at a 6 ft. to 7 ft. square iron plate at various ranges, each range correctly marked with a peg in the ground, is simple enough; but when it comes to obtaining records of pattern and penetration at targets from 30 to 80 yds. high in the air it is by no means an easy matter. I succeeded, however, in doing this after many failures and much wreckage of the apparatus I primarily employed.

My first object was to suspend a target with a surface of 7 ft. by 7 ft. to the string of a great kite, so that I could record the patterns of a gun on it at various heights. With so large a target as this I knew I could not fail to centralise a charge of shot somewhere on its surface, in such a way that I could obtain from the pellet-marks the usual selected 30-in. circle by which a gun's shooting is tested horizontally. I had to arrange my target so that its height above ground could be easily ascertained, and also varied as occasion required.

Besides this, I had to make a target frame which, when covered with a material to record the shot-marks, was not too heavy for a kite to lift ; and it was necessary to suspend the target so that it could be lowered and then raised again without winding in the kite. After a shot I had to contrive that the material recording it—that is to say, the covering of the target frame—could be taken quickly off and replaced when the target was lowered to the ground, previous to its being hoisted again for another pattern to be made. My second object was to raise a target which would give the penetrative force of a gun at various heights.

### Target for Testing Perpendicular Patterns of a Gun.

I had endless trouble. The first serious difficulty was to make a framework of thin laths which, when covered with some light material, would form a perfectly flat and level target to shoot at, and which would not hang sideways, or, as mine often did at first, turn upside down. In my earliest efforts I covered the target frame with sheets of white paper pasted together so as to fit the frame in one piece, each piece forming a surface 7 ft. by 7 ft.

I had several dozen of these sheets prepared, and intended to secure them, one by one as used, to the frame of the target with drawing-board pins. It was unfortunate that I did not have a trial of a sheet before making so many, as in that case I should have been saved much time and vexation. The first time the kite was flown, the target whirled round and careered about in mad fashion, loudly humming in the air as it did so, and away went its paper front at once, flying off in tatters, just like a flock of seagulls as a genial friend who was present remarked.

After this experience I decided that paper applied to the frame in this way was useless, especially as the same catastrophe occurred on every trial. This was a lesson. My next idea was that if I strengthened the paper front by nailing linen behind it over the frame of the target, then all would be well. This did not, however, have the desired effect, as the paper went off again on the wings of the wind, just as it had done previously when it had no protective backing of linen.

I now gave up all idea of paper, and had strips of thin linen sewn together so as to form a piece 7 ft. by 7 ft. I attached this piece to the edges and cross-pieces of the frame of the target by drawing-board pins, and on hoisting it 100 yds. high in a strong wind the linen front held perfectly and showed no sign of ripping off the frame as the paper had done. Still, however, it was most difficult to control the target and poise it aloft with sufficient steadiness to be a level mark to shoot at ; for it whirled about and entangled itself with the string of the kite in the most provoking manner. When lowered near the ground, and swinging at the end of its long cord, it ' took charge,' and was most unpleasant in its wild gyrations, and we had to advance and retreat and snatch at it till we secured it—an almost perilous performance. If we had allowed the target to drop of its own accord it would have been smashed to pieces.

Then the wind seldom suited. If we required a good

breeze to raise the larger kite and its heavy target of some 12 lb. weight, it was sure to be a flat calm, not a leaf stirring.

If a light breeze was wanted for the smaller kite that hoisted the penetration pads, then it blew a gale that uprooted trees.

Our surroundings were also at times a source of anxiety, especially if the wind shifted. There was an isolated clump of high trees which appeared a long way off when we sent the kite up. But the kite invariably made swoops in their direction, and twice, do what we would, it dropped the target gently into their topmost branches, which meant the best part of an afternoon wasted with men, ladders and axes to retrieve it.

As I had only certain days of leisure on which to carry out the experiments, it will be realised that they occupied some months before completion. However, the target was at length harnessed by means of cords to its corners, and weights and lines, so that it could be suspended as a level and stationary mark up to 100 yds. or more. With a small pulley lashed to the string of the kite, some score yards from the latter, and a long cord through it, the target could be quickly lowered or raised as wished, and down-haul lines held it steady when near the ground.

In order to regulate the height of the target, a cord was fixed to its centre that had small bunches of feathers lashed to it at intervals of 10 yds., the first bunch being 30 yds. from the target and the last one 140 yds. When patterns were being made, or penetration taken, an assistant held the particular bunch of feathers in his hands which determined the height required. He held the feathers level with his shoulder, and at the same time pulled the measuring cord tight, so that, standing beside him, the target could be slung at the exact height wished and directly above me.

I may here point out that when a bird is fired at perpendicularly, and is, say, 40 yds. above ground, it is 38 yds. or less from the cartridge in the gun, even in the case of a short man.

When plating a gun horizontally, with the feet against the mark which indicates the distance from the target, the arms, extended in the act of shooting, cause the muzzle of the gun to be considerably nearer the target than the feet.

Though this equally applies to perpendicular shots, there is the height of the body from the ground to the shoulder to be added as well. For this reason the assistant held the bunch of feathers at the height of his shoulder so as to equalise distances in horizontal and perpendicular shooting; otherwise the muzzle of a gun in the case of a perpendicular shot would be about 5 ft. nearer the mark than in a horizontal one.

Each 7 ft. by 7 ft. linen front, formed of several pieces sewn together and secured to the frame of the target, was taken off and replaced by a new one as required, the target being, of course, hauled down to the ground for this purpose after a shot. The amount of linen used would, I imagine, have covered a Guildhall banquet table many times over.

When the linen fronts were taken off the frame they were plainly marked to show at what height they were when struck by the pellets. They were then rolled up and afterwards examined, when the shot-pellets, in a selected 30-in. circle drawn on each linen front, were counted and recorded. If my field-glasses showed that a good pattern had been made on one side of the target, another shot was fired at the same linen front without lowering it to the ground, and sometimes two well-pelleted selected 30-in. circles were obtained on it which did not overlap. This saved much time and material.

Every target front before being shot at had a round patch of thin black gauze, the size of a dinner plate, pinned to it as a bull's-eye to shoot at, and temporary sights, breech and muzzle (previously tested for accuracy at a horizontal mark), were fixed to the guns so that the patch could be aimed at as with a rifle.

---

I soon found that, even when the wind was not sufficient to influence the bulk of the shot more than a few inches, I could not at 40 yds. centralise the pellets on the target if I placed the bull's-eye in its centre; for in such case, though I aimed directly at it, the bulk of the pellets were always a little beyond the patch. If the patch had been a stationary pheasant with its head towards me, I should, five times out of six, have placed the central pellets of the shot-charge in its tail, though in horizontal shooting no divergence of the kind was apparent. I corrected this by placing the patch at what to me, as I was standing, was about a foot forward of the centre of the target, in the direction a pheasant would be flying towards, if coming from the kite. This suggests that, besides the actual shooting allowance, from the shooter's point of view, that is necessary to kill a high pheasant, a slight additional forward allowance is required.

As I invariably stood and shot facing the kite, the target being directly above me, and as the wind, of course, blew from me or over the target towards the kite, I at first thought it was the wind alone which caused the shot-charge to strike beyond the bull's-eye—i.e., on that side of it nearest the kite.

This, however, was not the case, for on shooting at the bull's-eye, with my right or left shoulder towards the kite, i.e. standing sideways to the latter, the charge of shot equally went a little beyond the mark aimed at, though to one side in accordance with the force of the wind.[1] When I write that

---

[1] No doubt the reason is that the stock of a gun takes quite a different position when placed to the shoulder for an overhead shot to what it does for a horizontal one. In the former case the heel of the stock and the centre of the heel-plate rest against the unyielding bone of the shoulder, the toe of the stock being just clear of the shoulder. The result is, that when the gun is fired, i.e. directly the cartridge explodes, the toe of the stock is driven into the shoulder by the recoil, which means that the muzzle of the gun is, at the same instant, slightly depressed, and the charge of shot sent rather lower than the aim taken. In the latter case—i.e. in a horizontal shot—the toe and the centre of the heel-plate rest against the shoulder, and the heel of the stock is slightly clear of the shoulder. When the recoil takes place the heel of the stock is driven into the shoulder, and the muzzle of the gun is, thereby, slightly elevated, with the result that the centre of the charge is thrown a trifle high. When I wrote the first article on high pheasants I did not realise this, or why a gun shot a little low at a stationary bull's-eye straight overhead, but as soon as I suspected the probable cause, as above explained, I investigated the matter thoroughly, and at once set to work to prove the truth of it.

### THE HORIZONTAL SHOT

I fixed two 10-ft. poles in the ground a yard apart, and connected their tops with a cross stick. From the centre of this cross stick, to a peg below its centre in the earth, I stretched a length of cotton thread   At the height of the shoulder the cotton was previously cut in half, and the ends joined to a ring of thin wire, through which the muzzle of a gun could just be inserted. On firing the gun  horizontally, and standing in line with the upright thread, the lower portion of it, or its half between the ring and the ground, was always broken, thus showing that the barrels of the gun were jerked slightly upwards when the recoil occurred.

### THE PERPENDICULAR SHOT

The cross piece was now removed, and the tops of the poles were joined by the stretched cotton thread—the wire ring, as before, dividing it into separate lengths. On placing the muzzle of the gun through the ring, and then firing perpendicular shots, while standing in line with and below the thread, I found time after time, that the half of the thread which passed over and behind me was broken. This showed that the barrels of the gun jumped a little downwards,

the shot-charge went behind the bull's-eye I am treating the latter as if it were a pheasant coming overhead towards me.

I found that at 40 yds. high the shot-charge was considerably influenced by a strong wind, and in order to centralise it on the target I had to move the bull's-eye more forward, or to windward, as compared with what I had to do in a light breeze. A high and fast pheasant is difficult enough to kill without considering a wind allowance, which a shooter cannot well do at the moment of aiming ; still, this shows that if a wind exists,[1] especially a side one, it is a factor in the killing or missing of an overhead bird.

or away from the perpendicular, when the recoil took place ; and that, if an overhead stationary pheasant had been shot at, the charge would have been rather behind the bird towards its tail. From this it certainly appears that in the case of a high bird there is, as I have before pointed out, a forward allowance required of the gun itself, independently of the one naturally given to the bird by the shooter. Though this forward allowance that belongs to the gun cannot be exactly stated, it suggests that a more ample one than is usually given, as judged only from the pace and height of a bird, may meet with success when failures to kill occur.

[1] I naturally could not stand, when taking perpendicular shots, except with the wind blowing over me to or from the target in line with the bull's-eye. The wind was, therefore, always directly with or against the flight of a bird, if the bull's-eye had been one, according to whether the head of the bird was towards or from me.

A charge of shot is far more likely to intercept an overhead pheasant if it is flying directly with or against the wind, than it would if the wind was a side one, or across the mark ; i.e. in the case of the target at a right angle to the string of the kite, which, of course, could not occur.

# CHAPTER II

Patterns and penetrations of guns at various distances when fired horizontally and
perpendicularly, with deductions therefrom.

THE gun I employed in Series I., II., and III. gave a very regular
average pattern [1] at 40 yds. of 140 in the 30-in. selected circle;
which, with $1\frac{1}{16}$ oz. of No. 6, is, in my opinion, the most suitable
one for a good shot to use in game-shooting.   In all the shot-

## SERIES I

Average patterns of a gun in 30-in. selected circles (taken from 7 ft. by 7 ft.
targets) at different distances when shot horizontally and perpendicularly.
Ten shots fired for each average given.   Gun: modified-choke, making
an average pattern of 140 on a selected 30-in. circle at 40 yds. horizontal.
Load: powder, 33 grs. E.C.; shot, $1\frac{1}{16}$ oz. No. 6, averaging 287 to 289
pellets to the charge.

| Yards. | Horizontal. | Perpendicular |
|---|---|---|
| 30 | 220 | 207 |
| 40 | 140 | 132 |
| 50 | 114 | 103 |
| 60 | 78 | 73 |
| 70 | 29 | 25 |
| 80 | 11 | 9 |

[1] In all cases where the pattern of a gun is quoted, it represents the average
number of pellets that, in ten shots, show inside ten selected 30-in. circles
on a 6 ft. by 6 ft. horizontal target at 40 yds.; with $1\frac{1}{8}$ oz. No. 6 shot.

9

patterns and penetration trials, selected circles were taken. Though I do not approve of selected patterns as tests for a gun, they had to be used in the case of overhead targets, as these were not, at times, quite stationary. For uniformity, I acted in the same way in regard to horizontal shooting.

SERIES II

Average patterns on selected squares 10 in. by 10 in., taken from targets of 7 ft. by 7 ft., under the same conditions of gun, load, and number of shots as Series I.

| Yards. | Horizontal. | Perpendicular. |
|---|---|---|
| 30 | 60 | 52 |
| 40 | 33 | 27 |
| 50 | 20 | 16 |
| 60 | 14 | 11 |
| 70 | 8 | 7 |
| 80 | 5 | 4 |

When viewing the above patterns on the targets (Series II.), and regarding each of them as the bull's-eye or thickest cluster of the shot-pattern, it would seem as if at 40 yds. a perpendicular pheasant could not escape being killed. But this bull's-eye, or most closely pelleted part of the shot-charge—a selected one off a 7 ft. by 7 ft. surface, be it remembered—which we should like to place on our bird, is often on one side or other inside the pattern made by the gun, however excellent the gun or correct the aim of the shooter.

There are, besides, other matters to consider. In the first place, if the 10-in. squares were passing overhead like fast-flying high birds, from a fifth to a quarter fewer pellets would show on them, for reasons I shall presently give (p. 60). Then we have the pellets left that might kill at 40 yds. if they penetrated the vital parts of the pheasant. Shot-pellets do not, however, travel with equal force, as is evident from the considerable percentage of the charge that adheres to the first few sheets of the penetration pads (see notes after Series III.).

Finally, the superficial area of our selected 10-in. square (Series II.) is about three times larger than that contained in the outline of the under-surface of a cock pheasant. The average number of pellets out of the twenty-seven (Series II.) which are likely to strike with a killing velocity at 40 yds. perpendicularly, are not, therefore, more than four or five, and of this small number one or two would have to pierce, or strike so as to stun, vital parts of the bird to bring it down.

*Target for Testing Perpendicular Penetration of a Gun.*

To obtain penetration records I fixed nine Petitts's pads side by side in a frame of thin wood, so as to form a flat surface 28 in. by 30 in. A dozen of these targets were made, and the part of each target where the pellets were most numerous, after a series of shots, was marked with a circle of 1 ft. in diameter. The penetration of the pellets in these selected circles is given in Series III. Every target of Petitts's pads served twice by reversing it.

Sheets marked 'cracked through' were those in which light could be seen through the pellet marks when they were held against a lamp or a window. Sheets marked 'slightly cracked or indented' were the additional ones in which light could not be seen through the pellet-marks on them.

A Petitts's pad consists of forty-five closely pressed sheets of thick and hard brown paper, 10½ in. by 9 in.—made of a standard strength, and fastened together with wire at the corners.   They are very reliable for the practical testing of a gun's penetration when the comparison between the shots fired is taken from the same barrel.   Though I prefer straw-boards, each separate in a long box, for testing the penetration of shot, such a method was naturally out of the question in aerial shooting.

With a view to placing plenty of pellets on the penetration pads, a sequence of twelve shots was fired at each of the 40- and 50-yd. heights without lowering the targets to the ground; and, as the pattern was so scattered, twenty shots at each of the three higher altitudes.

### SERIES III

Penetration of a gun at horizontal and perpendicular targets, under the same conditions in the matter of gun and load as Series I.

| Yards. | | Sheets cracked through. | Additional sheets slightly cracked or indented. | Total number of sheets marked by pellets. |
|---|---|---|---|---|
| 40 | Horizontal .......... | 21 | 3 | 24 |
| | Perpendicular ...... | 17 | 3 | 20 |
| 50 | Horizontal .......... | 15 | 3 | 18 |
| | Perpendicular ....... | 10 | 4 | 14 |
| 60 | Horizontal .......... | 11 | 4 | 15 |
| | Perpendicular ...... | 8 | 4 | 12 |
| 70 | Horizontal .......... | 8 | 4 | 12 |
| | Perpendicular ...... | 6 | 4 | 10 |
| 80 | Horizontal .......... | 5 | 4 | 9 |
| | Perpendicular ...... | 3 | 2 | 5 |

By not less than three pellets in each sheet.

As I fired so many shots at the different heights, I always had plenty of pellets, even over a score at 80 yds., in the small selected circles to give a fair average record of penetration.   At 60 to 80 yds. no pellet had sufficient striking-velocity to stun or kill a perpendicular pheasant.   At 40 yds. perpendicular, a quarter of the number of pellets cracked only the first three or four sheets.   At 50 yds. one-third of them.   At 60 yds. one-half. At 70 yds. two-thirds ; and at 80 yds. no pellet adhered to even the first or outside sheet.

When sheets are given as cracked through by, let us say, ten pellets, this does not imply that the pellets actually penetrated ten sheets, as usually they did not penetrate more than half of them, though they cracked the others so that daylight could be seen through.   If No. 6 shot is to penetrate the thick skull of a cock pheasant, the strongest flying pellets of the charge will require to have a force of impact sufficient to crack (so that light can be seen through them) at least eighteen sheets of a Petitts's pad.   I ascertained this by fixing several skulls of freshly killed birds in the centre of a number of Petitts's pads, the latter being fastened together so as to form a flat target.

I commenced shooting at 50 yds. horizontal, and then, a yard at a time, decreased the range till I found the skulls were pierced or cracked by the shot.   At this point a small proportion of the numerous pellets that had struck near the skulls had broken from eighteen to twenty-two sheets of the pads, the distance being 38 yds.   I have not given penetration records at 30 yds., as at this height (even with No. 7 shot) the target, Series III., showed that the pellets had ample force to kill a pheasant as an overhead bird.

### *Deductions from Perpendicular Pattern and Penetration Tests (Series I., II., and III.).*

It is evident that a gun does not shoot so hard, and does not make so good a pattern, at a perpendicular mark, as it does at a horizontal one.    As a conclusive test of this contention, a dozen shots were fired at one of the 7 ft. by 7 ft. targets when 90 yds. high.    The shot-pellets could be distinctly heard to rattle against its tightly stretched linen front, but on lowering it to the ground only slight indentations were to be seen, and not a pellet had cracked the linen.    At 90 yds. horizontally, several pellets, out of a dozen shots fired, slightly cracked the linen, and a few even penetrated it.    At 122 yds. high, or the height of St. Paul's Cathedral (which is not 404 ft., as often stated), a considerable proportion of the shot-charge reached the target,[1] which in this case consisted of a large sheet of tin, because when only a few pellets struck it I could plainly hear them do so.

At this height it was curious to hear the long string of shot strike, there being approximately a fifth of a second between the arrival of the first and last pellets.    At 150 yds. the pellets did not reach the target.

Thinking that at this height I might not hear them if they did strike the tin, I brushed it over with whitewash, but, as a result of a score shots from a full-choked gun, no pellet-marks were to be seen.

I have proved by shooting cylinder-barrels, as well as modified and full-choke ones, with various sizes of shot at an angle of 45° over water and snow, that a gun will throw No. 6 to a range of 300 yds., or just about double the distance it attains when fired vertically upwards.    At both these maxima the shot-pellets are, of course, quite ineffective.

A pheasant at 80 yds. high is impossible, as the patterns and penetration results plainly show.    A pheasant at 70 yds. high is equally impossible.    At 60 yds. perpendicular, I do not believe a pheasant has ever been killed with an ordinary game

---

[1] Some pellets could be heard to strike the sheet of tin up to 145 yds.

gun, whatever the charge or boring. I have occasionally seen a partridge—a small and tender bird compared to a cock pheasant—knocked over at 60 estimated paces when flying low over roots, and when, of course, it offered its most vulnerable parts to the pellets ; but a perpendicular partridge at 60 yds. would be quite another thing, owing to various causes which I shall explain.

At 50 yds. high it is just possible a pheasant might be stunned by a pellet in the head, though this is unlikely to happen. At 40 yds. high a pheasant should be killed about once in half a dozen shots, or perhaps stunned by a chance pellet in the head. It might also, not seldom, be slightly wounded without stopping its flight. On the other hand, a low-flying pheasant crossing at 40 yds. may fairly often be killed. At 30 yds. high a pheasant should be killed every time, provided the aim is correct, even with a cylinder-gun.

In all cases I rely upon the bird being hit with a few pellets about the head and neck when I state it might be killed ; and I must emphasise the fact that these deductions are taken from patterns and penetrations obtained in perpendicular target practice, and not from a flying bird at the altitudes named. Anyhow, it is evident that, however accurate the aim, a really high overhead pheasant is a considerable more difficult bird to kill than the same bird would be at an equal distance from the shooter, but at a lower altitude.

———

It should be borne in mind that, in all the perpendicular shots given, the mark was stationary and not flying rapidly forward. For this reason more pellets are recorded on a target at an elevation of 40 yds., in a small space equivalent to the outline of a pheasant, than would have struck this space if it had been a fast-flying bird at the same height (see p. 60).

In the latter case, even with a correct aim and proper forward allowance, it may be taken that from one-fifth to one-quarter of the charge would pass behind the tail of the bird. A charge of shot leaves a gun in a detached column or stream, that is several yards in length by the time the first pellets of it reach a pheasant that is 40 yds. high.

A portion of this stream, that nearest the gun, consists of the weaker, slower, and most diverging pellets, or those which are the latest to arrive at the bird, or rather where the bird was. For instance, in Series I. the perpendicular pattern at 40 yds. is 132, and after deducting one-fifth of these there are only 106 pellets left in the 30-in. circle, of which not more than three, or at most four, would be likely to strike a pheasant in the body at a height of 38 to 40 yds.

If the shooter chanced to aim so far forward of his bird that the first half of the stream of shot passed in front of it, then a proportion of the last or slower part of the charge might arrive in time to score a kill; though, as far as the number and force of the pellets striking the bird was concerned, it would not be the same thing as if he had hit it with the first part of the shot-stream. From this it will be seen that in the case of a high-flying bird, or even a distant crossing one, it is impossible to use the entire charge of shot as a means of killing (see Stringing of Shot, p. 59).

In the case of a running bird on hard ground, a bird on the water or ice, or a bird flying directly towards, or from the shooter, the bulk of the shot-charge is, however, effective. If a bird is flying straight from you, any of the more central pellets of the charge have a chance of taking effect, as the slower ones would catch up the mark aimed at, in the same way as they all show when plating a gun horizontally at a target.

This does not, however, apply to a running bird, or a bird on the water, as in this case the aim should be taken at the ground or water about a yard short of the mark. The upper half of the shot-circle will then strike it and the lower half ricochet up to it. If a running bird or a bird on the water— I am alluding to a fair range—is shot at as if with a rifle, it often escapes, as most of the upper part of the circle of shot will pass above it, and only the lower part come chiefly into use.

In all my experiments I eliminated any wild or partially-off-the-target pattern, and fired another shot to replace it. With such a large target as 7 ft. by 7 ft. I had no pattern up to a height of 50 yds. that was not satisfactory enough for obtaining a 30-in. selected circle, as I could not well miss the mark, or fail to place the bulk of the shot-charge on some part of it. At 60 yds., however, it was sometimes difficult to say where the pellets were thickest or thinnest in number, or whether the central ones were placed on the linen front ; and at 70 to 80 yds. this difficulty was greatly increased.

With a modified-choke barrel I had very few bad patterns up to 50 yds. perpendicular, though they were naturally very open at altitudes over 40 yds. With full-choked guns (I tried three) some strange experiences and very poor patterns occurred, even at 40 yds. At 50 yds. high I more than once, with a full choke, failed to place a quarter of the charge on the target, big as it was.

———◆◆◆———

# CHAPTER III

Experiments with large shot—The comparative velocities of small and large shot in relation to a forward allowance for game—The boring of guns in regard to killing high pheasants—On hearing the shot strike the game—The distortion of shot-pellets.

## SERIES IV

Experiments with large shot, relative to shooting high pheasants.

| Size of shot. | Load of shot. | Horizontal. | Perpendicular. | Variation. |
|---|---|---|---|---|
| No. 3 ...... | $1\frac{1}{8}$ oz. ...... | 117 ....... | 102 ....... | 15 |
| ,, 3 ...... | $1\frac{1}{16}$ oz. ...... | 110 ....... | 96 ....... | 14 |
| ,, 4 ...... | $1\frac{1}{8}$ oz. ...... | 138 ....... | 120 ....... | 18 |
| ,, 4 ...... | $1\frac{1}{16}$ oz. ...... | 133 ....... | 118 ....... | 14 |

I. Average patterns in selected 30-in. circles at 40 yds. on targets 7 ft. by 7 ft. Ten shots fired with each load. Gun : full-choke, bored for No. 4 shot.

---

| Size of shot. | Load of shot. | Horizontal. | Perpendicular. | Variation. |
|---|---|---|---|---|
| No. 3 ...... | $1\frac{1}{8}$ oz. ...... | 76 ....... | 68 ....... | 8 |
| ,, 3 ...... | $1\frac{1}{16}$ oz. ...... | 72 ....... | 65 ....... | 7 |
| ,, 4 ...... | $1\frac{1}{8}$ oz. ...... | 91 ....... | 82 ....... | 9 |
| ,, 4 ...... | $1\frac{1}{16}$ oz. ...... | 87 ....... | 80 ....... | 7 |

II. Average patterns in selected 30-in. circles at 40 yds. on 7 ft. by 7 ft. targets. Only six shots fired with each load as, from a game-shooting standard, it was evidently a waste of time and ammunition to complete this section of Series IV. Gun : modified-choke, bored for No. 4 shot.

### *Note on Series IV.*

IN this series there is only one pattern that, from a target point of view, might possibly kill a perpendicular pheasant at 40 yds. This pattern, from a full-choke gun, consists of an average of 120 pellets in the 30-in. circle at 40 yds. perpendicular, with 1⅛ oz. of No. 4 shot—a heavy load.

An outline, to scale, of the under-surface of a cock pheasant as it would appear to the shooter when above him, was drawn in the centre of each of the ten separate patterns that collectively gave the average of 120 pellets. In this way it was easy to see how many pellets would have struck each bird, supposing a bird to be in the centre of every selected 30-in. circle. Twenty-one pellets would have hit the ten birds. Three birds would have been struck by three pellets each, five by two, and two by one pellet each. No bird would have been hit over a vital part.

If we deduct from the average pattern of 120 pellets only one-fifth of their number to represent those that would pass behind a fast-flying overhead bird at 40 yds., however correct the aim, our pattern is reduced to ninety-six. In such case not more than an average of one pellet to each bird fired at could be expected, and many would not be struck at all!

At a height of 50 yds. No. 3 and No. 4 shot in the full-choke guns gave patterns that were, if possible, even more useless for game-shooting. I tried No. 3 and 4 shot, because I have met shooters who reserve a few cartridges loaded with these sizes for a stand where pheasants fly exceptionally high. From the results I obtained with Nos. 3 and 4, as shown in Series IV., I am confident it is a great handicap to a shooter to use such large sizes at very high birds.

The patterns made by No. 4 (No. 3 need not be considered), with a full-choked gun, at perpendicular targets at 40 yds. were often so open or patchy that a pheasant might have flown through them in two or three places without being struck, even allowing that all the charge reached the bird's altitude at the same instant, which, as I have before pointed out, does not occur.

A charge of No. 4 shot has a superior striking-velocity to a charge of No. 6, but this attribute is of no use in helping us to kill our game at a long range unless we also have a good pattern. Striking velocity is all very well if one chance pellet happens to penetrate some vital part of a bird, but with the very scattered pattern No. 4 gives, even in a full-choke, such a piece of luck may not occur once in a score shots. If we are to place sufficient pellets on a pheasant 38 to 40 yds. high to kill it with No. 4 shot, then we require a pattern in the 30-in. circle of at least 165 at 40 yds. horizontal. This 165 would give a perpendicular pattern in the selected 30-in. circle of about 150 at 40 yds. ; and, after deducting a percentage of the slower pellets of the charge, a fast overhead bird at this height should be struck by an average of five to six pellets.

There are 183 pellets in $1\frac{1}{16}$ oz. of No. 4 shot, and 194 in $1\frac{1}{8}$ oz. In the first case, supposing a pattern of 165 at a horizontal target at 40 yds., there would only be eighteen pellets outside the 30-in. circle, and with $1\frac{1}{8}$ oz. there would be twenty-nine. No full-choke gun ever made—and no other form of boring need be considered if No. 4 shot is used—could, however, put every pellet of $1\frac{1}{8}$ oz. of No. 4, less twenty-nine only, inside a 30-in. circle at 40 yds. horizontal, and its failure would be more pronounced at the same target and distance when perpendicular.

As a gun, even a full-choke, cannot nearly do what I have described as a necessity if No. 4 shot is used, its pattern is too scattered to kill a pheasant at 40 yds. overhead, except by the merest chance. The conclusion I come to when I hear of pheasants being killed at a height of 40 yds. with No. 3 or No. 4 shot is—that the birds are nearer 35 than 40 yds.

Allowing a correct aim, what we require is a pattern that will hit our high bird with a good many pellets, so that some of them may have a chance of entering its vital parts, which parts, taken collectively, do not represent a surface of larger area than a small playing-card.

An ounce of No. 7 has plenty of penetration and pattern to kill at 30 yds. high and more, but might sometimes spoil a pheasant at a usual range, which is nearer 25 yds. than 30.[1] If the cartridge is properly loaded, No. 7 lies very compactly, which has not a little to do with the force with which shot is projected from a gun. It is, I believe, far the most effective size for ordinary high pheasants, and I put down such birds as 30 yds. above ground, which is a good deal higher than most trees you are likely to see in a day's outing.

Even for birds of exceptional heights, or from 38 to near 40 yds., I should pin my faith to 1 oz. of No. 7 and 34 grs. E.C., or the equivalent in any other good nitro powder.

The striking velocity of No. 7 at 40 yds. is 629 ft. per sec., and that of No. 6 is 649—a difference of no account whatever from a killing point of view. The number of pellets in an ounce of No. 7 is 340, and there are 270 in an ounce of No. 6. The extra seventy pellets in No. 7, above No. 6,

[1] There are, however, only thirty-six more pellets in an ounce of No. 7 than there are in 1⅛ oz. of No. 6. The latter charge was commonly used a few years ago, though it was not then said to plaster a bird, at a fairly close range, with too many pellets !

might be most useful in the matter of hitting the head or neck of a high bird.

One of the best shots in our islands uses 1 oz. of No. 8 for especially high birds only, and kills them as cleanly and consistently as anyone could wish. When using Nos. 8 or 9 for shooting snipe, have not many of us been surprised at the long distance at which a chance wild-duck can be brought down dead with such small shot?

*The Comparative Velocities of Small and Large Shot in Relation to Killing Game.*

It is a common error to suppose that a small size of shot, as No. 7, is considerably slower in reaching a bird than a large size, such as No. 3 or No. 4. At 35 yds. No. 7 would only require about 3 ins. more forward allowance at a crossing bird than No. 3: a trifling amount when, perhaps, the forward aim given is several feet, and the killing diameter of the shot-circle is some 3 ft.

As the difference in the time of arrival of No. 3 and No. 7, at an object 35 yds. distant, is practically the same as the difference in time of arrival of No. 3 and No. 6 at an object 40 yds. away, I will take the two latter sizes for comparison, as 40 yds. is the usual range in gun-trials.

Time of arrival of No. 6 shot at 40 yds. = ·1378 sec.
,, ,, ,, No. 3 ,, ,, = ·1329 ,,
Difference = ·0049 ,,

A bird crossing at a rate of 40 miles an hour has a speed of about 60 ft. per second. Therefore, in the time saved by No. 3 shot, as compared with No. 6, the amount would be (60 × 12 = 720 ins.) × ·0049 sec., or—

$$
\begin{array}{r}
720 \\
·0049 \\
\hline
6480 \\
2880 \\
\hline
3·5280 \text{ ins.}
\end{array}
$$

which is just 3½ ins.

To give No. 6 this 3½ ins. of extra forward allowance, the muzzle of the gun would only require a fraction of an inch of additional lateral movement—an amount too insignificant to consider, and beyond calculation on the part of the shooter.

As the forward edge of the pattern of the gun with No. 6 shot is only 3½ ins. behind the forward edge of the pattern as made by No. 3, the difference is trivial as far as game-shooting is concerned, as a variation of 3½ ins. could not influence a kill or a miss at a crossing pheasant.

The difference in time, for instance, between the arrival of No. 4 and No. 7 shot at a bird as much as 40 yds. distant, is so small that it need not be considered, and at ordinary ranges of about 25 yds., the time of arrival of the two sizes is practically the same.

That large shot, as No. 4, travels much faster than a smaller size, as No. 6 or No. 7, and that for this reason the aim need not be taken nearly so far in front of a crossing bird, is a fallacy that is often accepted as a fact by shooters.

*Full-Choke, Modified-Choke, and Cylinder-Guns in connection with Shooting High Pheasants.*

I found no great difference between a gun with full-choked barrels giving a pattern horizontally at 40 yds. of about 200 in the regulation 30-in. circle, and barrels giving a pattern of 150, when both were tested at heights of 40 and 50 yds. The pellets scattered with the one gun almost as much as with the other ; though the full-choked barrels, chiefly owing to thick clusters here and there, together with their usual fault of pellets in twos and threes touching one another, certainly had an advantage in the number of shot-marks in the selected 30-in. circle.

It is doubtful if a full-choke gun will kill very high pheasants better than one that makes a pattern of 140 to 150, and we all know that the former is much the less effective weapon to use at ordinary ranges by reason of its close and usually irregular shooting. At a height of 40 yds. the full-choked guns sometimes gave very patchy patterns, and shot generally with less regularity than did a modified-choke.

It is an undoubted fact, and a great handicap to a shooter who uses one, that, owing to the jostling of the shot in the barrel, a full-choke seldom shoots straight to the mark, however correctly it is aligned. This, I have found, will occur even when the gun is fixed in a rest to hold it absolutely true and steady.

For instance, when testing a full-choke for its pattern, it is most difficult to place the bulk of the shot-charge within a previously drawn 30-in. circle. The result is, that to obtain the stated pattern of the gun a selected 30-in. circle has to be taken after each discharge, here or there wherever the pellets show thickest upon the surface of a 6-ft. square target, the centre of the pattern in this selected circle being, perhaps, a couple of feet away from the centre of the 30-in. circle at which the gun was directed.

With a cylinder-gun, and more or less with an improved cylinder, the pattern can, time after time, be taken from a 30-in. circle drawn round the bull's-eye aimed at. A selected pattern is then not necessary—and such a pattern is always an incorrect test in regard to the accuracy of a gun's shooting to a given point. As I have said, penetration is of no service without a good pattern, nor is a good pattern of use if the penetration of a gun is really weak. A good pattern is, however, the first necessity, as with well-made guns and cartridges penetration is generally satisfactory.

I also fired many shots with a true cylinder-gun at 40 yds. perpendicular, a gun with an average pattern of 105 to 107 ; and from the results, with $1\frac{1}{16}$ oz. No. 6, it might be considered useless at this height. At 30 yds. high, the height of an ordinary tall pheasant, the cylinder-gun, allowing the aim to be correct, would, however, easily kill its bird ; and, indeed, judging by the patterns of both, the difference at this elevation between a modified-choke gun that makes 140 on the horizontal target at 40 yds. and a cylinder that averages only about 107 is surprisingly small so far as a useful killing pattern is concerned.

Though the one gun, of course, puts more pellets in its bird, the other puts in quite sufficient to kill at a height of 30 yds. For instance, at a horizontal target at 30 yds., ten shots fired, the cylinder placed an average of 186 pellets in the selected 30-in. circle with $1\frac{1}{16}$ oz. No. 6, and the modified-choke under the same conditions made an average of 220 ; at the perpendicular target the cylinder at 30 yds. averaged 174 and the modified-choke 207.   The cylinder had a considerable advantage in one way, as its pattern was larger and more evenly spread, especially round the outside of the 30-in. circle.   It would have been the best gun of the two for a moderate shot to use at fairly high pheasants, as its wide and well-distributed pattern allowed the most latitude for an incorrect aim.

From the above it will be realised that at 30 yds. perpendicular, if a shooter aims correctly, he could scarce fail to kill his bird, for even with a cylinder-gun his shot-pattern at the height given is not far short of that of a full-choke at 40 yds. horizontal.

### On Hearing the Shot-Charge Strike the Bird.

A curious question, and one that relates to the distance of a bird from the gun, is how high or far is a pheasant when one hears, or fancies one hears, the shot strike it.

If this sound is really heard, and is not some form of echo, which I believe it to be, it cannot be caused by the pellets striking the soft body of the bird, but something hard, such as the quills of the larger wing-feathers.   I have, however, more than once picked up a bird which a friend declared he had heard his shot strike, and yet none of the quills of the wing-feathers were damaged.   Shot passing through the webs of the wing-feathers would make no noise that could be audible to the shooter.

Shooting at a large sheet of tin—a very resounding substance —and with the aid of a special stop-watch, I make the interval between the discharge of a gun, fired by an assistant close to me, and the returning sound of the pellets striking the tin as three-tenths of a second at 70 yds., and a little less at 60 yds. ; at 50 yds. the interval is too short to be recorded. At 40 yds. there is still an interval, but so slight a one that it is very difficult to detect it. At ordinary game-shooting ranges of from 25 to 28 yds., I consider it is impossible for the quickest hearing to detect the instantaneous sound of a few pellets of shot rattling against a bird, before the rattling reverberation caused by the gun's discharge has ceased in the ear. Anyone who takes the trouble to calculate the velocity of shot and sound, at 25 to 28 yds., will easily realise there is not time to do so. The curious thing is, that if a bird is purposely missed, or there is no shot in the cartridge, the same noise, echo or whatever it is, may be heard that gives the impression of shot striking the game! Here is a story I can vouch for the truth of, which is a good example of what imagination can do in regard to the supposed hearing of shot striking.

The not uncommon discussion of this subject came up one night after dinner in the smoking-room of a country house among a party of shooters, and it was agreed to test the question the following day, the host's gun and cartridges to be used so that all might be the same for every one.

The next morning a salmon-line was attached to the legs of a cock pheasant taken from the larder, and the bird was thrown over the yard of the flagstaff on the cricket-ground, where it hung dangling in mid-air. Twenty-eight yards distance was measured. The host fired first. The guests heard nothing, and, accusing their friend of having made a clean miss, much amusement was caused. Then the guests, A, B, C, D, each had a shot in turn.

A heard nothing. B heard something, but could not say whether the sound was caused by his shot striking the bird or not.   C and D both said they heard their shots strike distinctly, and implied that anyone must be more or less deaf who didn't do so, but were careful to explain that their hearing was exceptionally acute.   So the matter rested, two for, two against, and one doubtful.

The same evening consternation ensued, for the head-keeper, who had fetched the cartridges from the gunroom in the morning, came with a long face to his master to explain that they were taken out of a small card box, the lid of which he had just noticed was marked with the words ' Loaded with fine sand.'

It so happened that the schoolboy son of the house was an ardent collector of natural history objects, and had especially ordered a few cartridges to be loaded with fine sand, instead of shot, with a view, during the past summer, of shooting, without spoiling as specimens, some very fine dragon-flies that haunted the lake in the grounds !

---

Up to a range of 30 yds. it is doubtful if the striking of the shot is ever heard, as it would reach the bird, and the sound of its striking return to the shooter, practically during the noise caused by the explosion of the cartridge.   As a bird is not like a reverberating sheet of tin, the farther off the former is from the shooter when he kills it, the less is he likely to hear the very few pellets of shot that strike it, especially as the striking-force of the latter is decreased according to distance.

Anyhow, if a shooter insists that he heard his shot-charge strike his bird, he may usually feel assured it was beyond fair killing range.

## *The Distortion of Shot-Pellets.*

It is a sorry thing to see the shape of shot-pellets after being fired from a gun. If they could only leave the barrel, where all the damage to them occurs, in their proper spherical form the patterns and penetration of our guns would be greatly improved. As it is, if examined with a magnifying glass, they are more like brickbats and rough chunks of iron slag in shape than anything else. Their very irregular outlines, whether hard or softer shot be used, must check their velocity to a great extent, as well as make their line of flight deviate from the true direction ; but whether their distortion causes them to diverge more in perpendicular shooting than in horizontal I cannot say. Possibly it does.

A good example of the distortion of shot is to fire a charge at some cakes of soap or into a mound of snow. After extracting some of the pellets, cover one side of a piece of glass with gum and sprinkle them on its surface. Then throw the picture on a white sheet with a magic lantern.

# CHAPTER IV

I HAVE given the theoretical aspect of killing high pheasants at various altitudes, as judged by the results obtained from patterns and penetrations carefully recorded on perpendicular targets. I will now deal with the killing of high pheasants from a more practical point of view, which view, I must say, does not entirely corroborate my theoretical deductions.

On an estate I know of, there is a small, disused factory, the chimney of which is exactly 40 yds. high. It has been accurately measured, as being a constant source of interest, because no shooter has ever been known to kill a pheasant, and no one has ever seen one killed, that was flying level with the top of this chimney! Yet, during a day's shooting, many scores of birds have passed it. The chimney stands in a valley, between low wooded hills, off the sides of which the birds rise. Though good game-shots have often tried to do so, no one can say that a pheasant has ever been killed that was flying overhead level with the top of the chimney.

As it is only fair to give both views of the 40-yd. high

pheasant, here is a contrary one to the above. In the park at Cobham in Kent there are some wonderful ash-trees, probably the tallest timber in our islands, though nearly approached by some beeches at Ashridge Park in Hertfordshire. Mr. Elwes, in his very fine volumes on Forestry, gives the height of some of the ash-trees at Cobham as being from 138 ft. to 144 ft. When at Cobham lately, I carefully verified the heights of some of them, and my measurements agreed with those given by Mr. Elwes. Over these trees pheasants have not been shot, but over others at Cobham of the same kind, measured as 128 ft., pheasants have many times been killed.

The owner of Cobham, who has a great experience of shooting, assures me this is the case, which puts the matter beyond all possible doubt.

The height of a pheasant above ground is, it may be said, invariably over-estimated, though the height of a tree, chimney, or church tower, may as easily be under-estimated. When cricket is dull at Lord's, which it frequently is, and shooting is perhaps a relieving topic, sportsmen are apt to notice the massive chimney so plainly visible opposite the entrance gates. I have often heard the question asked : ' Could you kill a pheasant at the top of that chimney ? ' The minority of shooters will say : ' No ; I don't think I could, as it must be quite 40 yds. high.' But the more usual reply that I have heard is : ' Well, a bird at the top of that chimney would be a real good one, but I think I could kill it sometimes.'

The manager of the electric works to which the chimney belongs has given me accurate details of it. It stands 244 ft. 9 ins. above ground, or 81 yds., so it is evident that a pheasant flying level with its top would be far beyond the reach of a game-gun—nearly twice as far, it may be said. The lower edge of the ornament of the chimney, from the top of the latter, is 20 yds., though it looks, owing to its height above ground, far less than a score yards. An overhead pheasant merely the length of this part of the chimney above a shooter could not be called a very low bird!

The solidity of the chimney referred to takes away from its real height and deceives the eye, which is no doubt the reason why it is often said not to be higher than the height at which a pheasant could be killed. The chimney near Lord's is 14 yds. higher than the Monument to the Fire of London, the total height of which is 67 yds., and if you stand near the base of the latter you would never for a moment imagine a pheasant could be killed at its summit! Nelson's Column, including the statue, is 54 yds., and the Duke of York's is 46 yds., with the figure. Both these columns are good examples of heights in relation to high pheasants.[1]

Again, if you go into the inclosure round the north side of St. Paul's Cathedral, and look up at the pigeons fluttering about the cornice of the main building, it would seem as if they could not be killed with a game-gun ; and yet this cornice is only 100 ft. above ground. This gives a good idea of the distance at which a bird 33 yds. overhead appears, compared to what it does when seen horizontally. A pheasant could easily be killed at the cornice of St. Paul's, and perhaps, by a rare chance, at the top of the Duke of York's Column ; but not at the top of Nelson's Column, and most certainly not at the top of the Monument.

It may be noted that the capital of the Duke of York's Column (in which the railings are fixed) is only 36 yds. above

---

[1] All books of reference differ as to the heights of these monuments, but the details given above may be taken as correct.

ground, though it looks as if a pheasant flying past this part of the building would be out of range.

———————————

It is rather the fashion among some game-shots to shoot at a high pheasant as directly above them as they can, even bending backwards as they do so.  They have not, however, any chance of a second barrel at a really high bird, if it is missed when so straight overhead as the position referred to implies.

It is often argued that if a shooter leans backwards and fires at an overhead pheasant after it has slightly passed him, he is more likely to score a kill by reason of the shot-pellets entering the body of the bird under the ends of its breast and neck feathers.

This is a curious supposition, as in the case of a bird flying directly over his head, the shooter—if his spine did not break —would require to bend backwards till his gun pointed at an angle behind him of about 45°, before the shot would enter under the feathers, which overlap on the body of the bird like slates on the roof of a house.  The farther an approaching overhead pheasant is allowed to pass behind the shooter, the less vulnerable does it become, and the more are its vital parts protected, including head, neck, and heart ; whilst the parts it might be only wounded in are chiefly exposed to the gun.

The best angle, and at all events it is one theoretically correct, at which to place the shot-charge so as to kill an advancing high bird, is to meet, i.e., in some measure intercept it with the shot, and hence to fire at it a few yards farther in

D

front of you than is the general custom.[1] You then also
have a chance of a second barrel, should you miss with
your first, before the bird is past and done with.

We all know the high pheasant that appears to be sailing
towards one with a slow and easy flight, with apparently plenty
of time to shoot at it ; and we all know the same bird when it
is just overhead, and seems (for it does not really do so) to
double its pace and pass like a flash, giving scarce time to take
an aim, which, by the way, is then often a consciously incorrect
one ! A pheasant does not fly like a wild duck, with its neck
stretched out as straight and stiff as the neck of a bottle : for
when in full flight it carries its neck slightly folded near its
body. You can test this by laying a pheasant sideways on a
table, and placing its head and neck in the line of what its
horizontal flight would be if alive—and as it would naturally
carry it.

If you go a few yards away and kneel down, you will then
see the body of the pheasant in the position it would appear
as a straight overhead shot. You will notice that the neck of
the bird is a good deal protected by its breast and crop. You
will also realise that in this position its breast-bone and the
thick pectoral muscles on either side of it, are shields that
guard its vital organs, such as the heart and lungs. These
organs and the head and neck are more open to damage from
shot-pellets if the bird is fired at when a few yards in front,
than if it is taken when straight overhead.

If a pheasant is 28 yds. above ground and flying towards
a shooter, and he fires at it 10 yds. in front of him, it is only
4½ ft. farther away than if it were shot at directly overhead, and

---

[1] See remarks (p. 74) on the much harder blow that shot-pellets give an
approaching bird as compared to one that has passed.

has to pass through a wider stream of shot. In the former position the bird looks the easier shot, whether it is or not, and this suggestion in itself may give the confidence that ensures a kill.

I have alluded to the forward allowance, as it is generally termed, which is universally insisted on as being always required in a more or less degree, if a shooter is to kill a high and fast pheasant, whether the bird is overhead or crossing. The question of forward allowance is a subject which I will enter into later (see p. 72).

Some shooters declare they aim a certain mentally and momentarily arranged fixed distance in front of a bird, and then pull trigger. Others maintain they swing the gun with the bird, and just as they pull trigger jerk the muzzle forward of it, and fire without checking the motion of the gun as it travels in line with the mark. Whether a shooter acts and handles his gun as he imagines he does when shooting at fast-flying birds, I have great doubt. He may kill his bird, but whether he kills it in the way he thinks he does is another matter.

An old friend of mine, the best shot at high pheasants I ever saw—I have seen him kill forty in succession, in forty single shots, without a miss—many times assured me that he directed his gun at the head of his bird, and, with a quick swing in line with the object, pulled trigger, with the muzzle of the gun still covering its head. This friend always fired at high birds more in front of him than anyone else in the line of guns. I noticed it was his constant custom; and the success with which he killed his game on these occasions bears out what I have said on the subject of taking a high bird slightly as an approaching shot, rather than as one directly overhead.

It is safe to say that when a shooter fires behind his bird, this result, five times out of six, is caused by his dwelling on the trigger.

————————

There are two reasons, more or less independent of the shooter, why very high pheasants are difficult to kill. One reason is, that they usually, when shot at, have only the sky as a background, and are not near the tops of trees, which might otherwise help to indicate their position, height and pace.

The other reason is, that when several come together, their pace often varies, the strongest birds flying fastest. If a shooter, therefore, has been killing the slower birds with a well-judged forward allowance, the faster ones—though they may not appear to him to be flying at a speed above the others—may easily be missed through shooting behind them.

In covert-shooting, a very high pheasant is nearly always the result of the shooter standing far below the bird, as, for instance, in a valley between hills. When passing from the crest or side of one hill to another, a pheasant seldom takes an upward flight, though it often seems to do so ; it merely pursues a horizontal course, though sometimes a slightly downwards one—the most difficult of all shots if the wings of the bird are rigid—to the place where it intends to alight ; and it just depends on the depth of the valley in which the shooter is standing, or the height of the ground from which the bird rises, whether it is in or out of range.[1]

[1] Among many other places where I have seen pheasants fly very high off wooded hill-sides, I may mention as examples Bishopswood, Benacre, Berkeley, Gwernyfed, The Hendre, Harpton, Londesborough, Margam, Mulgrave, Penrice, Penrhyn, Powis, Rokeby, Roundway, Stoke-Edith, Walcot, and Wallop. I consider the birds that fly across the deep valleys at Bishopswood, Mulgrave, and Walcot are consistently the highest pheasants throughout a day's shooting

If a pheasant, with stiff and motionless wings, planes down at a good height over sloping ground, it is usually an impossible shot to make any certainty of; and I am almost grateful when a bird of this kind favours someone else rather than myself!

If the bird I describe passes overhead it should not be so hard to bring down as it generally proves to be. If, however, it presents a side-shot sloping downwards, and its flight can be observed, it is easy to realise the great difficulty of then killing it, for a lateral swing is as much out of the question as is a forward aim.

As I have said, high horizontally-flying birds always appear to be travelling slowly towards you, though not so if viewed sideways, as when passing over other guns in the line of shooters. This deceptive flight, as regards pace, is the most frequent cause of missing, through the aim not being taken nearly forward enough.

Even in a flat country, a pheasant rising well back in a large field of roots, as in partridge-driving, will often mount high in order to avoid the shooters, whom it can plainly see between it and the point it wishes to make for. It then gives a good example of its rate of flight, slow as it often looks; as, should it be flushed at the same time as the partridges, it always leaves them far behind, even though its progress, as it climbs upwards, does not equal its velocity when flying horizontally and nearer the ground.[1]

I ever shot at. The tallest pheasants I know of are at Harpton, at a rise called Harley's gorse, where the birds come off the top of a high hill and then pass above the shooters standing in a valley below them.

[1] On several large estates round Thetford—probably the best natural game and inland wild-fowl district in our Islands—I have seen pheasants fly higher out of large fields and heaths, during partridge-drives, than in perhaps any other part of England. As examples: Elvedon, Euston, Buckenham, Lyndford, Didlington, and Merton may be quoted; and, though some distance from Thetford, Gunton should be included, as the birds at this place are equally good ones.

I may mention that a grouse as easily outstrips a partridge in flight as does a pheasant.

It is curious to record that among the fifty or sixty exceptionally high pheasants shot by myself, or by my friends, which I have had through my hands for examination during the last few years, at least twenty of them were actually killed by the shock caused through their violently striking the ground when falling from a great height.

They were all examined and reported on by various expert taxidermists, and it was proved that a considerable percentage of the birds which were seen to crumple up in the air, as if killed at that moment, were only stunned by pellets which had partially flattened against the bone of the head, but had not penetrated, the real cause of death being the smash up of the chief organs of the bird by its contact with the ground.

A pheasant struck by the shot in the same way as many of these very high ones were, would have presently recovered, and either flown away or run like a hare, if it could have been gently placed on the ground, instead of falling on it and then rebounding like a heavy stone.[1]

### *The Influence of Gravitation in Relation to a Game-gun.*

In theory, gravitation is not supposed to influence a charge of shot when fired perpendicularly, more than when it is fired horizontally, the central attraction of the earth being the same in both cases. Nor if shot is fired from, let us say, a balloon, and straight down towards the earth, does gravitation appreciably assist its pace of flight, for the shot travels much

---

[1] The position and effect of the shot-pellets that struck a score of these high birds will be described in the next chapter.

faster by the energy of the explosion than it would fall by gravitation. When the shot has lost this energy it merely falls by the force of gravity.

Here is, possibly, an example of this contention, and one that tends to show, as I have described in perpendicular target practice, that from 145 to 150 yds. is the limit, whether straight upwards or straight downwards, that a charge of No. 6 shot can reach before its acquired velocity is expended.

On some steep cliffs on the Yorkshire coast, known to be 450 ft. high, myself and others, when staying with the late Lord Londesborough for partridge-driving, used to have one afternoon at the rock-pigeons, as they flew in to roost in the cliffs from the adjacent country. Our stands consisted of small walled inclosures built on the very verge of the cliffs ; and as the pigeons, often in hundreds, flew to their holes and ledges in the face of the cliffs, they were usually underneath us, and hence we often shot straight down at their backs. On the seashore near the base of the cliffs, and immediately below us, a dozen or more men were placed to keep the pigeons on the move by firing guns, as well as to gather the birds we killed.

The first time I visited the cliffs for this most difficult of all shooting, I allowed many pigeons to pass without firing at them, as I was afraid I might injure the men below me on the strand, who were frequently in a direct line with the birds. I, however, need have exercised no such care, as several of these men told me afterwards that, though they had assisted in the sport for many years, no one had ever suffered the least harm. To use their words, ' the shot fell soft as rain.'

The explanation is that when a charge of shot from a gun is fired straight downwards it gradually loses, through atmospheric resistance, nearly all its momentum before it

has completed a distance of 150 yds., and that after it has
lost the velocity conveyed by the powder, it then falls the
rest of the space by gravitation, and thus drops gently
to the ground.

———

[It would naturally be thought that when shooting straight
downwards, the speed of gravitation should be added to the
speed of the shot-pellets, as bestowed by the energy of the powder.
As an analogy, if a man is standing on the stern of a steamer
travelling slowly through the water at three miles an hour,
and he runs forward towards the bow of the ship at ten miles
an hour, he is then moving at thirteen miles per hour. If he
ceases running forward, his pace is again three miles an hour.
For the sake of illustration, the speed of the ship may here
represent the speed of gravitation, and the pace of the man the
speed of the shot-pellets.

From this point of view, if a charge of shot is fired straight
downwards, gravitation should increase its speed, for the pellets
should travel at the rate produced by the explosive energy of
the powder plus the speed of gravitation, until the resistance of
the atmosphere had absorbed the energy that started the shot-
charge on its course, and then it should continue to fall at the
speed caused by gravitation only.

Shot-pellets fired straight downwards should, therefore,
travel at the speed produced by the powder-energy plus the
speed given by gravitation, and shot-pellets fired straight
upwards, at the speed produced by the powder-energy minus
the pull of gravitation. In the former case one would imagine
gravitation should increase the velocity of the shot. In the
latter, the pellets are struggling against the pull of gravitation

throughout their entire flight, and for this reason should lose their velocity at a considerably shorter distance than they should if fired straight downwards.] [1]

## Perpendicular v. Horizontal Shooting.

It is well known that a charge of shot does not travel nearly so far perpendicularly as it does when fired at an angle of 45°. The atmospheric pressure retarding the pellets is practically the same in both cases, and the constant pull of gravitation towards the centre of the earth should also be equal, whether the pellets travel vertically upwards or horizontally.

The reason why a charge of shot fired horizontally travels so much farther than one fired vertically, is because when it is fired at a fairly high trajectory its course of flight is a parabola. If shot-pellets reach a height of, say, 150 yds. vertically, they, of course, fall straight down. When they are projected to the distance of 150 yds. at an angle of 45° they cannot drop straight down from their highest elevation, but continue their flight in a long curve, till they reach the ground. [2]

If a gun is shot vertically upwards, i.e., at an angle of 90°, and is then gradually directed downwards, away from the perpendicular, and fired at intervals till an angle of 45° is

[1] The three preceding paragraphs merely give a theoretical view of the question of gravitation in connection with a charge of shot fired vertically downwards.

[2] If a modern rifle is aimed at an angle of, say, 45°, the spin given to the bullet causes it to act differently to a spherical projectile. With a rifle-bullet, the angle of descent from its highest elevation is much shorter, or more abrupt, than the angle it takes to reach this point. In the case of a round cannon-ball, or a shell from a mortar, either of which a pellet of shot may be taken to represent in miniature, the angle of ascent to the highest point, and the angle of descent therefrom, do not differ to nearly the same extent as occurs with a rifle-bullet.

reached, each shot will have an increased range, the longest being at 45°, or about double what it was at 90°. Below 45°, the range would decrease till (supposing the muzzle of the gun was level with the ground when it was shot) it was practically *nil* when the gun pointed to zero, or parallel with, and resting on, the earth.

# CHAPTER V

I WILL now give details of the effects and position of the shot-pellets that caused the death of some exceptionally high pheasants. Though I have accurate records of over fifty collected during several years past, if I describe a score of them it will, I think, be sufficient for my purpose, which is to show that the killing of a very high bird depends greatly upon chance, accurate though the aim of the shooter may be. The birds were unusually tall ones ; and the few of them I shot myself I can answer for as being, to all appearance, quite out of the common run of even very high ones. These I killed in places where pheasants are often allowed to pass over without being fired at, as beyond the reach of a gun.

The pheasants sent to me I received from friends, experienced shooting-men, who well know the difference between an exceptionally high bird and a high one. Many of their letters commenced in much the same way: such as, ' I am sending you the highest bird I ever shot in my life,' or, ' A bird leaves for you to-night that I really think is the highest I ever saw shot here,' or, ' I saw —— kill a pheasant to-day that I did

43

not think any gun could possibly bring down, and am posting it to you.'

When writing my thanks I always inquired if the bird received was shot dead in the air, or if it fell with a broken wing. When the latter case was admitted, I sent the bird to the kitchen without forwarding it to be reported on by one or other of the taxidermists I at the time employed. I only retained those birds which I was positively assured were shot dead, and which were usually described as falling ' like a stone,' or else as ' crumpled up in the air.'

I cannot, however, put any of the exceptionally high birds which I shot myself, or which my friends shot and sent to me, as having been over 40 yds. ; so I will take the average height at 40 yds. We will see what a game-gun can do with a perpendicular pheasant at 40 yds. or 120 ft.

I can say nothing about the boring of my friends' guns ; but as I never meet anyone in these days who uses a full choke in game-shooting, I should imagine they would make ordinary patterns of about 140.

The larger proportion of the specimen birds sent to me came from the west of England and from Wales, because in these parts the country is hilly, and the stands for the shooters are often in valleys between the hills.

I did not receive a bird from Norfolk, and in Norfolk I personally know only two places where pheasants fly high in covert-shooting.[1] As I have said, pheasants often fly high in a level district out of large level fields of roots, or from heaths, when being driven forward with partridges, but these high birds generally fly at much the same altitude, and, though,

---

[1] At Taverham, near Norwich, where there are hills, or what pass for hills in Norfolk ; and at Ken-Hill in the north of the county.

they afford most sporting [1] and tall shots, I cannot say I have ever seen one that I should regard as beyond the reach of a gun, or at a height even of 40 yds.

## SERIES V

*Twenty exceptionally High Pheasants and how they were killed.*

1. Cock bird struck by two pellets. One pellet hit the head near the left ear, but did not fracture the bone. The other pellet struck the right side of the breast, and, passing through the pectoral muscle for a distance of $1\frac{1}{2}$ in. at a depth of $\frac{1}{4}$ in., passed out again. The bird was stunned by the pellet that struck its head, and was killed by its violent contact with the ground.

2. Cock bird struck by five pellets. One pellet lodged between the skin and the flesh of the inner surface of the right thigh, inflicting only superficial injury. Three pellets struck the right side of the breast, near the middle line, and one of these would have reached the heart if the bird had been nearer the gun, but, as it was, it only partially penetrated the pectoral muscle. The remaining pellet fractured the base of the skull, and, causing hæmorrhage of the brain, killed the bird. No. 7 shot was found in this specimen.

3. Hen bird, hit and killed by one pellet. This struck just beneath the left eye, and passed out above the right eye. It did not touch the brain, but the skull was fractured.

4. Hen bird, struck by five pellets—three pellets on the right side of the under surface of the body, and one in its centre.

---

[1] I use the word ' sporting ' here only in reference to a ' sporting chance ' of killing; for with all driven game it is a question of skill with the gun, rather than actual sport with it.

These four pellets inflicted merely superficial flesh wounds, but the fifth penetrated the soft edge of the breast-bone, and, reaching the heart, killed the bird. This bird was killed with No. 7 shot.

5. Cock bird, struck and killed by one pellet. This bird seemed to have been flying with its head and neck drawn in upon its shoulders. The pellet grazed the left shoulder, and then slightly scratched the left side of the neck. It next entered under the bird's chin, and, passing through the brain, it just perforated the top of the skull, where it remained imbedded beneath the skin.

6. Hen bird, struck by four pellets ; two pellets caused superficial flesh wounds on the left side of the breast ; one pellet struck the neck, but did very slight injury to it ; one pellet passed through the thin edge of the breast-bone, and killed the bird by penetrating the heart.

7. Cock bird, struck by three pellets ; one pellet caused a superficial flesh wound in the centre of the breast ; one pellet cracked the great arm-bone of a wing. The third, which killed the bird, penetrated the pectoral muscle at the side of the breast-bone and reached the heart.

8. Hen bird, struck by two pellets ; one pellet passed through the skin of the neck, just missing the windpipe. The other pellet struck, but did not fracture, the base of the skull, and was found partially flattened beneath the skin. The bird was stunned by this pellet, and killed by violent contact with the ground.

9. Hen bird, struck by three pellets ; one pellet penetrated the thin end of the breast-bone and entered the abdominal cavity ; one pellet caused a superficial flesh wound on the right side of the breast. The third pellet was found partially flattened

beneath the skin below the left eye. This pellet did not fracture the bone of the skull, but stunned the bird, which was killed by violent contact with the ground.

10. Cock bird, struck by two pellets ; one pellet pierced the windpipe, and one pellet reached the heart by passing through the breast-bone a little to the left of its centre, and this pellet may be said to have killed the bird.

11. Cock bird, struck by six pellets ; four pellets caused only superficial flesh wounds on the breast ; one pellet cracked the shin-bone of the right leg, one pellet entered under the head near the base of the lower mandible, and, lodging in the brain, killed the bird. No. 4 shot was found in this bird.

12. Hen bird, struck by two pellets ; one pellet fractured one of the smaller bones of a wing, and the other pellet bruised, but did not fracture, the bone of the skull below the left eye. This pellet stunned the bird, which was killed by its violent contact with the ground.

13. Cock bird, struck by five pellets ; two pellets caused superficial flesh wounds on the left side of the breast, one pellet penetrated the pectoral muscles and breast-bone, and reached the heart. Another pellet fractured the lower mandible, and the fifth pellet struck the left side of the head near the eye, and, passing through the bone, lodged in the brain. This is the only bird in the series that received two fatal wounds, and the size of shot found in it was No. 7.

14. Cock bird, struck by two pellets ; one pellet fractured the hand-bone of the left wing, and the other pellet penetrated the pectoral muscle at the right side of the breast-bone, and, lodging in the heart, killed the bird.

15. Hen bird, struck by three pellets ; one pellet entered the abdominal cavity to one side of the end of the breast-

bone; another pellet slightly fractured the small end of the
breast-bone.　The third pellet struck, and partially flattened
against, the bone of the skull below the right eye, where it
remained beneath the skin.　It did not fracture the bone, but
stunned the bird, which was killed by its violent contact
with the ground, or, perhaps, the branch of a tree, as it was
much lacerated.

16. Hen bird, struck by two pellets; both pellets imbedded
in the vertebræ of the neck on the right side.　Though the
bird was much smashed internally by its violent contact with
the ground, it may have been killed in the air, but was more
probably stunned by the shot, and killed by the fall.

17. Cock bird, struck by five pellets; three pellets caused
superficial flesh wounds on the breast, not penetrating more
than $\frac{1}{4}$ in. through the pectoral muscles; one pellet entered
the abdominal cavity near the smaller end of the breast-
bone.　Another pierced the pectoral muscle about $\frac{1}{4}$ in. on
one side of the breast-bone, and, lodging in the heart, killed
the bird.　The pellets found in this specimen were No. 7.

18. Hen bird struck by two pellets; one pellet cracked the
shin-bone of the left leg, and the other, glancing for nearly an
inch along the skin of the neck, entered the head beneath the
chin, and, passing through the brain, fractured the top of the
skull, and killed the bird.

19. Cock bird, struck by four pellets; one pellet slightly
cut the skin of the left side of the neck, inflicting no real
injury.　The other three pellets were within 1 in. of each other,
just outside the left side of the breast-bone.　They had all
travelled towards the heart through the pectoral muscle, and
were found nearly touching it.　The shock of these three
pellets brought the bird down, but it is an open question

whether they caused its death or not. It was much smashed internally through violent contact with the ground.

20. Hen bird, struck by three pellets ; one pellet passed for ɪ in. in length and at a depth of ¼ in. through the left side of the breast ; one pellet lodged in the flesh of the right thigh. The other pellet bruised the head near the right eye, but did not fracture the skull or remain in the skin. It, however, stunned the bird, which was killed by its violent contact with the ground, or, perhaps, the branch of a tree or a stone, as it was internally much lacerated.

### Deductions from Series V.

ɪ. It should be borne in mind that broken-winged birds, which might have fluttered down from a great height with no other damage, were not included in those I sent for examination. The pheasants reported on were, what is termed, shot dead in the air to all appearance, though several of them, without the shooter being aware of it, were merely stunned by pellets that did not penetrate vital parts, and were really killed by the force with which they struck the ground.

2. That though four or five pellets may strike a very high pheasant, it is a mere chance if one of them enters a vital part with sufficient force to kill.

3. That to have a good chance of killing a very high pheasant at least seven or eight pellets should strike it, since, on an average, not more than two of this number are likely to hit in vital places.[1]

---

[1] If we wish to kill our game, we have to kill it in the best way we can, and small shot, such as No. 7 (as I have explained), gives us the greatest chance of doing so, as it is more likely to hit in vital places than a larger size. No. 3 or No. 4 is far too uncertain to use as a means of killing a high pheasant—a really high one, that is to

E

4. That a very high pheasant may be struck by four or five pellets without causing it to fall, or even wounding it but slightly. In the examples given, it happened that, with only two exceptions (one doubtful, No. 16), one pellet killed each bird. We have, however, no estimate of the number of very high birds that are hit, but not killed, because a 'lucky' pellet does not penetrate a vital part.

5. It will be noticed how few of the birds were hit in the wings, legs, or near the tail. The answer is, that if they had been chiefly hit in these parts they would have either flown on, or perhaps fluttered down, and could not then have been regarded as shot 'dead in the air,' and, therefore, I should not have received them, or sent them to be reported on.

6. Very few birds were hit in the neck, and only one killed (doubtfully, No. 16) in this way. The neck of a pheasant is very tough, and about as thick as a man's thumb. If you fire at a piece of wood of this thickness, and 3 in. or 4 in. long, at 40 yds. above you, you might not put a pellet in it once in a score shots, and even if you did, allowing the piece of wood to represent its neck, it does not follow that you would penetrate this sufficiently to kill the bird.

7. A very high pheasant has many chances in its favour, and I am glad it has. In the case of the twenty birds reported on (a small proportion, no doubt, of the very high ones shot at), twenty-one pellets were fatal out of sixty-two that struck.

8. Taking an ordinary high pheasant as being 28 to 30 yds. above the shooter, even if only five or six pellets strike

say. There is much exaggeration in the theory that No. 7 severely wounds a high bird if it is only struck in the body. This is more likely to occur with a pellet of No. 4 than with a pellet of No. 7 (see p. 52).

it (though there would be nearly double this number with a correct aim), these five or six might have plenty of velocity to cause a fatal wound, without striking the head or neck; whilst in the case of a very high bird, as shown, only one or two 'lucky' pellets would be likely to have force to kill, and then only if they chanced to penetrate a vital part.

*On the Shock given to a Bird when Struck by the Charge.*

In connection with Series V. the question of the 'shock' given to a bird when a number of pellets strike it in the body may be considered. If mere shock would kill a really high pheasant, then I should have had some specimens sent to me that were killed by being hit in the body only, without showing any pellets in vital places. But, as it was, each bird I received had a pellet or two in some vital part, and these pellets were responsible for its death. Ordinary overhead pheasants, at from 25 to 28 yds. high, that are struck in the body by, perhaps, six or seven pellets, large or small, with none in the head, heart, or neck, would usually fall dead at once from the shock, for at this distance they would penetrate deeply, and the bird, though no pellet reached a vital part of it, would be knocked over just as if it were a wounded one on the ground that was killed by a blow from a stick.

I have, however, examined winged pheasants caught by a retriever two or three days after a cover-shoot, at which no birds were above an ordinary height, and found four or five pellets in their bodies, sometimes even several of No. 4, and yet these birds, when captured, were actually feeding with the uninjured ones in the woods !

It is an erroneous and rather fanciful idea that if a few

pellets of No. 7 shot strike a high pheasant in the body, missing a vital part, the bird suffers greatly and must eventually die therefrom. I find, as the result of much investigation of killed and wounded birds, that this is not the case, and that the damage caused to a high bird by such small shot hitting it in non-vital parts is far less than generally supposed.

As we cannot make a certainty of placing pellets in vital parts of high birds, however true the aim or whatever shot we use, we are obliged to load our cartridges with a size of shot that gives us a pattern that helps us to do this as far as possible.

For this reason, we unavoidably strike our high pheasant with several pellets that cannot kill it.

Many writers advocate the use of No. 3 or No. 4 for very high birds, and describe the wonderfully long shots which they have occasionally made with these sizes.

I have already explained (p. 19) what a great handicap it is to a shooter to use No. 3 or No. 4.

The pattern is very inferior, even in a full-choked gun, at 40 yds.; and in practice on game No. 4 has little superiority in penetration over No. 6 or 7, whatever may happen with pads of paper.

Some of the high pheasants I received for examination had two or three pellets of No. 4 in their breasts or sides; but it was noticeable that these had not penetrated deeper than the smaller sizes of shot had done in the case of other high birds sent to me.

It is an old fallacy that a pellet of No. 4 will go through and through a high pheasant, and, therefore, bring it down dead when the bird is hit only in the body, and that for this reason No. 4 has a great advantage over No. 6 or No. 7, which may, it is said, have no effect when they strike the body of the bird, but only when they penetrate to a vital place.

If a high pheasant is hit in the head, neck, or heart, by one pellet of No. 4, then down it comes, just as it would if hit in the same way by a pellet of No. 7; but judging from the many birds I have examined which were struck in the body by several pellets of No. 4, no one need imagine that a bird so hit with this size is sure to be killed, either by shock or penetration, as this is very far from being the case.

My experience, especially with wild-ducks, is, that two or three pellets of No. 4, unless they hit a vital part, will seldom penetrate the flesh and muscles of the body so deeply as to cause immediate collapse. I have recovered ducks days after they were wounded with No. 4 shot, very much alive and with several pellets in the body. When afloat with a punt-gun, I have often knocked over, though not winged, geese with B.B. shot, which I have afterwards found in their breasts and sides, and sometimes retrieved the birds two or three days later, and had a hard pull in a boat, and several shots with a shoulder-gun, before I could do so. A smaller size of shot would have probably killed these birds at the time they were fired at, through some of the then more numerous pellets striking them in the head and neck. As I have previously pointed out, the velocity of small and large shot, as used on game, shows only a slight difference. From its larger surface a No. 4 pellet meets more resistance from the plumage of a bird, and often, as I have constantly seen happen, only penetrates a short distance, through driving the feathers in front of it into the wound it causes; when a pellet of less diameter might have passed through the feathers into the flesh, and possibly reached a vital place. As an analogy : if we take two bradawls of the same size and weight, the one having a point a third smaller than the other, and drop them from the same height, so as to each fall side by side on a soft piece of wood, the one that has the smallest point will penetrate the deepest of the two.

I will add that I certainly have seen some very high pheasants killed with 1 oz. of No. 4 shot and an extra charge of powder, but never with any certainty or regularity. These birds were no doubt hit only in vital places, and could have been brought down just as well, and more frequently, with No. 6 or No. 7.

# CHAPTER VI

Target-pheasants, and how they would have been killed if they had been live birds flying overhead—The stringing of a charge of shot when fired from a gun.

THE pheasant (Fig. 1) offers only three small vital parts to the gun (especially small to hit if it happens to be a really high bird). These are the head, the neck, and the heart. In all three cases, taking an overhead pheasant as 40 yds. high, a pellet must strike with great force to penetrate vital parts (especially to the heart), unless it chances to enter under the chin of the bird, or pass through an eye, or cut the windpipe in the neck. It may, however, stun the bird by hitting the skull without fracturing the bone, as exemplified in Series V.

If a stag is shot through the heart, it will always spring forward about 20 yds. before it falls, though a flying bird struck in the same way drops instantly. In the former case the muscles of the limbs act after the animal is killed. In the latter, as the bird cannot use its legs, and has no contact with the ground, it at once collapses.

Fig. 1 represents the under-surface and partial anatomy of a large cock pheasant. The bird is denuded of its feathers, and shows the target it actually presents to the shooter as it approaches him, just previous to passing in a direct line over his head. I have preferred a cock in order to give the gun as good a chance as possible, as a hen, with its smaller outline, would be struck by fewer pellets.

This sketch may be consulted in connection with the records

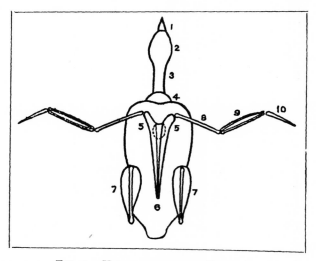

FIG. 1.—UNDER-SURFACE OF PHEASANT.

1. Bill. 2. Head. 3. Neck. 4. Crop. 5-5-6. Breast-bone. 7-7. Shin-bones. 8. Great arm-bone. 9. Forearm. 10. Hand-bone. The dotted oval under the breast-bone is the heart. The breast-bone and pectoral muscles are thickest below and round the heart, and protect it, as well as other vital organs, including the lungs and the larger blood-vessels, from outside injury.

given of 'exceptionally high birds, and how they were killed,' Series V. It may also be referred to in relation to the experiments described in the following series.

## SERIES VI., VII., VIII

These give the number of shot-pellets that would strike the under-surface of a straight overhead (stationary) pheasant at different heights, taken from selected patterns of a gun on 7 ft. by 7 ft. targets at the same elevations.

In this series, pellets that would have struck the wings of the birds are not included, as in such case they are not killed in the air, but are probably recovered a quarter-mile distant by a dog. Nor are the one or two pellets marked that would have struck the legs, as a broken leg, unfortunately, does not stop a bird's flight.

Gun : average pattern of 150 on a selected 30-in. circle at 40 yds. horizontal ; load, 35 grs. E.C. $1\frac{1}{16}$ oz. No. 6, averaging 287 to 289 pellets to the charge.

What may be called the shot-patterns to be seen on the pheasants in Series VI., VII., VIII. were obtained by etching with a diamond, on a piece of glass, the outline to scale of the under-surface and partial anatomy of a large-sized cock bird, of which the diagrams in this series are reproductions one-seventh of the actual size. By placing the figure of the bird, as etched on the glass, over a selected 30-in. circle on one of the 7 ft. by 7 ft. linen targets, the pellet-marks could be seen through the glass, and their respective positions accurately dotted with ink on its surface.

The ink-spots were copied on the reduced sketches and then wiped off the glass, and other patterns were obtained from other linen target-fronts in the same way, till all the patterns required were copied on the reduced sketches of the birds, as seen in Series VI., VII., VIII. The shot-marks on the sketches are drawn of large size so as to show plainly where they would have struck.

It is worthy of comment that the average number of pellets that struck the live birds in Series V. at 40 yds. (estimated) and the pellets that would have struck the target-birds in

Series VI. at 40 yds. (actual) were very similar. In Series V. the birds were hit in vital places, or stunned; otherwise they would not have been killed, and I should not have had them for examination. In Series VI. the birds were seldom struck in vital places, and they would not have been sent to me, as possibly not one of them would have been killed. This shows what a number of shots may sometimes be fired at a pheasant 40 yds. high without bringing it down.

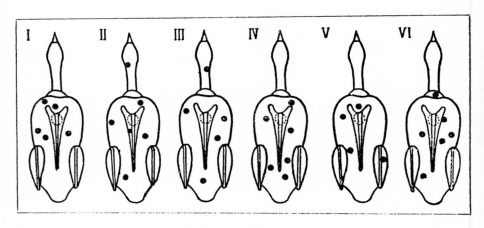

FIG. 2.—SERIES VI

Height, 40 yds.—No. 1. Superficial injury.   No. 2. One pellet on the head, which might have killed or stunned the bird if it had sufficient force.   Other wounds superficial. No. 3. One pellet on side of neck, which might possibly have caused serious injury, though not immediate collapse.   Other wounds superficial.   No. 4. No vital parts struck.   No. 5. No vital parts struck.   No. 6. No vital parts struck, unless the pellet to one side of the breast-bone had slanted towards the heart, and had force enough to penetrate the pectoral muscle protecting it.

SUMMARY.—One vital wound (No. 2), one doubtfully vital wound (No. 3). The remaining thirty pellets would not have stopped the flight of the birds.

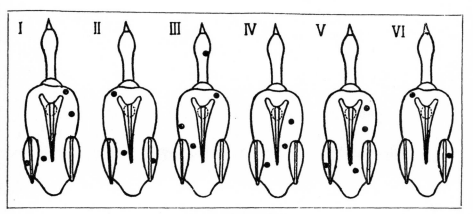

FIG. 3.—SERIES VII

Height, 50 yds.—No. 1. Superficial injury.   No. 2. Superficial injury.   No. 3. One pellet struck the head, but at 50 yds. perpendicular could not be expected to fracture the bone or stun the bird, though it is just possible it might do so.   No. 4. Superficial injury.   No. 5. Superficial injury.   No. 6. Superficial injury.

SUMMARY.—Twenty pellets struck the birds, but only one of these (No. 3) might, very doubtfully, have caused injury sufficient to kill the bird.

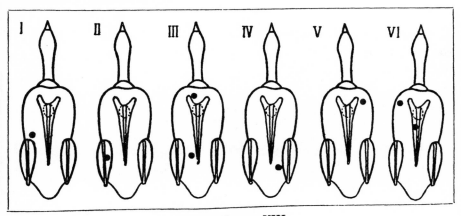

FIG. 4.—SERIES VIII

Height, 60 yds.—No. 1. Superficial injury.   No. 2. Ditto.   No. 3. Ditto.   No 4. Ditto. No. 5. Ditto.   No. 6. Ditto.

Summary.—The six birds were struck by eight pellets, none of which would have scored a kill.

In connection with Series VI., VII., VIII., I must repeat that if the 30-in. selected circles on the 7 ft. by 7 ft. targets, from which the shot-patterns on the birds were taken, had been travelling fast overhead at fifty to sixty miles per hour, like flying pheasants, they would not have shown so many pellet-marks as they do (see below, ' The Stringing of Shot ').

For the same reason, the birds in the diagrams would have fewer pellets on them, and one pellet should be deducted from each. If we deduct one pellet from each bird, then Series VI. suggests that at a height of 40 yds. there is a fair chance of killing a pheasant. At 50 yds., Series VII., there is practically no chance of doing so, as at this height a pheasant would seldom be struck by more than two pellets, and these would not have sufficient force to penetrate a vital part, even if (once in a score times) they happened to strike above it.

At 60 yds., Series VIII., not one bird in six might even be hit ; and if a pellet had the luck to do so, it could not have a striking-velocity to cause injury.

## The Stringing of Shot.

Though I have alluded to this subject more than once in connection with killing fast-flying crossing birds, I will now refer to it again, and more fully.

The reason of the stringing of a charge of shot, when fired from a gun, has never been explained, or why it should fly forward like a squirt of water from a garden syringe.

The length of the string or column of pellets from a cylinder-barrel is longer than it is from a choked one, though, up to 30 yds., the cylinder has generally a higher velocity than the choke, as it does not distort the pellets to the same extent as the choke does.

In theory, the slower pellets of the column, or those nearest the gun, have a velocity that enables them to reach, at 40 yds., a fast overhead or a crossing bird, before it can fly clear and escape them, on the principle that the slowest pellets of the charge would travel up this distance much faster than the time the bird would take to fly its own length.

This theory, common to text-books on gunnery, is not, however, borne out by practice.

From observation and experiment I do not believe that more than, if, indeed, as much as, three-quarters of the long column of shot is of any service to a shooter in killing a high pheasant or a distant crossing one.

The slower or hindmost pellets of the shot-column all show on a stationary target, as they cannot fail to reach it ; but a considerable proportion of these do not reach a fast crossing bird before it has flown clear of many of them, if it was missed ; or, if it was killed, before they can come up to the position the bird was in when it fell to the shot.

When grouse-driving, I have often killed the foremost bird of several crossing me at a long-range down-wind, and then, an instant after, seen another drop dead that was some yards behind the first one at the time the latter fell.

At near 40 yds. the few most divergent pellets of a charge of shot may be some 20 yds. apart, and it might be supposed that one of these stray pellets may sometimes have the luck to strike a following bird in the head and kill it. This cannot be the explanation, as I have many times seen a bird quite 6 yds. behind the leading one that I shot, crumpled up and shot all over with apparently as many pellets, judging from the number of feathers that flew off it, as the one that dropped in front of it at almost, though not quite, the same instant.

On such occasions there seems little doubt that the leading bird is knocked down by the first or strongest part of the column of shot, and that the following bird is killed by flying into the slower half of the column that comes up later into the position the first bird occupied when it was killed.

It will be realised that both birds are really killed when in the same position, though one after the other at a fractional interval of time. As the leading bird naturally falls forward on being shot, if crossing with a fresh wind, the space in the air between it, as it drops, and the second bird, is, to all appearance, the same as when the one bird was following the other previous to the gun being fired.

Again, many shooters can remember that after missing the first bird of several crossing at a long range, they have seen another fall that was coming up some yards behind it. It does not at all follow that the shooter aimed so very much behind the first bird as to kill the second with the front pellets of his shot-charge, as he more likely struck it with the last or slowest pellets.

I merely describe here what I have often witnessed ; though theorists may argue that after a leading bird has been killed, the entire column of pellets will have passed the line of flight of a bird following at some yards distance, before the latter could have a chance of flying into any part of the column. In this case, as in various others I could name dealing with guns and shooting, theory and practice do not agree.

A few years since, I tested in a simple manner the question whether the fast and slow pellets of the shot-column could strike a crossing pheasant at practically the same moment ; or whether a proportion of them only reached the original position of the bird after it had fallen, or had flown forward. In fact, whether the slowest pellets of the column of shot trailed up, figuratively speaking, so that they could kill a second bird that had flown into the position previously occupied by one some yards in front of it.

I placed a 5-ft. post in the ground and fastened a thin metal disc, 8 in. in diameter, at its top, and, of course, facing the shooter. Over the front of this fixed disc, and close to it, I suspended a second one exactly the same size, held in position by a little notched stud of steel, so arranged that the least pressure against the front disc, such as the contact of a few pellets of shot fired from a gun, released it at once and allowed it to fall down—its pace of fall being increased by a length of rubber cord stretched from a hole in its lower edge to a peg in the ground. Both discs were whitewashed as required.

When shooting at 40 yds. almost as many pellets showed on the underneath or fixed disc as on the front one !

This result plainly showed that after the front disc was hit and had dropped clear of the fixed one behind it, the slower pellets of the charge came up and struck the latter. These slower pellets might have killed a following bird, but they would not have been up in time to have helped in the killing of the first bird, as represented by the front disc.

As the front disc could not be set free from its catch—when the first few shot struck it—quite instantaneously, it received more pellets in proportion to its size than if it had been a pheasant flying rapidly across the target.

---

The longer the distance of a crossing or overhead bird, the longer the column of shot sent up by the gun, and the less the number of killing pellets available to intercept its flight, and the greater the number that come up after the bird is killed or has flown on.[1]

[1] If a charge of shot is fired at Pettits's pads at 40 yds., a large proportion of the pellets penetrate, or crack, only from a quarter to half as many sheets as those pellets which penetrate or crack the greatest number of sheets.

This is conclusive evidence that the striking velocity of a considerable portion of a charge of shot is much less than that of the fastest flying, i.e. hardest hitting, part of it.

The pellets of lower velocity that only penetrate or crack through from a quarter to half as many sheets as do the pellets of high velocity, naturally strike with considerably less force than the latter, and it stands to reason travel slower, and lag behind the others. Thus, the faster pellets in front and the slower ones that follow them, string out, according to distance, into a long detached column, that travels in this form from the gun to the bird.

The late Mr. R. W. S. Griffith, a very able experimentalist with guns, tested the stringing of shot by means of a thin circular disc 12 ft. in diameter. Mr. Griffith shot at the upper part of the face of this disc at 40 yds., when it was revolving by machinery at 200 ft. per second, and found the shot-charge made a longitudinal pattern on it of from 10 ft. to 12 ft. in length.

This extended pattern proved beyond question that instead of the charge striking instantaneously, all in a cluster, it arrived in a string, the slower pellets of which struck the surface of the revolving disc some time after the fastest ones.

The average velocity of No. 6 shot may be taken as 600 ft. per second for the fastest or first pellets that reach a mark at 40 yds. The rotating speed of the disc should, therefore, also—only this was not possible—have been 600 ft. per second ; as, to obtain a pattern showing the total length of the shot-string, it is obvious that the part of the surface of the disc shot at should move past the shooter, as he fires at it, at the same velocity as the shot-pellets travel up to it.

With the disc revolving at 200 ft. per second, Mr. Griffith obtained an extended

From this it will be seen that a considerable proportion of the charge of shot cannot be utilised for striking a high or a distant crossing bird, and this is another reason why it is so hard to kill; though you may shoot your gun at 40 yds. at a stationary target and wonder if even a jack-snipe could escape the close pattern it makes.

The stationary target does not, however, show the stringing of a charge of shot.

pattern of 10 ft. to 12 ft.; but if it had been revolving at 600 ft. per second, the pattern, or string of shot, from the first to the last pellets, would have been nearly three times as long, or, as Mr. Griffith pointed out, about 30 ft. In the case of a rotating disc—or for that matter a long flat target, if it could be arranged to move longitudinally at a sufficient speed—the pattern of the shot-stream would always be lengthened just in proportion as the velocity of the shot-pellets exceeded the speed at which the disc revolved, or at which the target passed in front of the gun.

A pheasant crossing overhead, or to one side, at 40 yds., flies, when there is no wind, at a rate of about 60 ft. per second, and travels nearly 9 ft. during the time occupied by the fastest pellets of the charge of shot in reaching it.

If a crossing pheasant at 40 yds. requires an allowance of from 8 ft. to 9 ft. under the above conditions, it is clear that the slowest pellets of the string of shot could not come up to the bird [should it not be killed] before it had flown clear of them: i.e. beyond the position it was in when the fastest pellets reached it. Anyhow, it is well to give a high, or a distant, crossing pheasant a rather more ample forward allowance than at first sight might appear necessary; as if the fastest pellets of the shot-charge did happen to pass in front of it, then slower pellets might come up in time to kill.

If, however, the forward allowance is not sufficient, then, of course, the first part of the shot-charge, and the slower part that follows it, will both pass behind the bird.

What percentage of the fastest portion of the shot-string strikes a crossing bird, and what percentage of the slower portion of the shot-string comes up too late to be of service to the shooter, is, however, beyond conjecture.

———————◆◆◆———————

F

# CHAPTER VII

The penetration of shot-pellets on live birds at various heights—The difference in the apparent size of a pheasant when seen overhead and horizontally—How to kill a pheasant overhead—How to kill a high pheasant that has passed behind the shooter. The position of the arms and hands when swinging a gun on game.

I HAVE given the patterns and penetration of guns fired at targets at various altitudes. I have also described how a number of high pheasants were actually killed, Series V., and again, Series VI., VII., VIII., how high pheasants might be killed, or missed, when treated from a target point of view.

I will now deal with the last experiment I carried out, which was to test the penetration of shot-pellets on pheasants at different heights. The results are curious, and, to a game-shooter, rather surprising.

The birds in this experiment, Series IX., were full-grown cocks, which were taken separately from the pen they had been kept in, and each in turn killed by hand a few minutes before it was hoisted up by the kite.

They were, therefore, practically live birds as regards the penetration of the shot-pellets that struck them.[1] Previous

---

[1] They were, however, in one way more vulnerable to the shot than if they had been live birds on the wing. The latter would have had their breast-feathers laid compact and close to their bodies, and for this reason their plumage would have offered a little more resistance to the pellets. As the dead birds were suspended directly above the shooter, the shot struck them just as it would have done live birds in the same position—a very usual one to kill them in, and one that resembles that of the stationary birds as regards the angle and effect of the shot striking.

to shooting at the birds I tested some of the cartridges I was about to use, and found that at Petitts's pads they showed excellent penetration at 40 yds. horizontal.

The pheasants were attached, one at a time as required, to a small framework of cane. Their wings, heads, and bodies were fastened to the framework by wire, in an extended position as if they were flying, so that each bird, when suspended to the kite-string, offered the usual target presented by a high pheasant passing directly above the shooter.

The three heights, 40, 50, 60 yds., were represented by three lengths of cord, accurately measured to correspond. For instance, if a bird was to be suspended at a height of 40 yds., then it had the 40 yds. length of cord attached to its legs, and was sent aloft till the cord was stretched tight to the hand of the person who held its lower end, and who stood beneath the bird, and close to the shooter.

The birds suspended at the higher elevations were treated in the same way, the longer cords being, of course, employed to determine their altitudes.

During the trials, the wind was slight, and the birds hung so steadily that they would, to all appearance, have been easy to hit with a rook-rifle. With a gun it seemed impossible to avoid ' plastering ' them all over, especially as, in order to make certain of placing plenty of pellets in them for the test, so many carefully aimed shots were fired at each bird without lowering it to the ground. The details of what happened are given on the next page.

## SERIES IX

No. 1.—Stationary pheasant at a height of 40 yds. Six shots fired (over 1700 pellets).

RESULT.—Twenty-four pellets lodged in the bird.    One pellet in the heart ; one pellet broke the arm-bone of the right wing ; one pellet passed through the gullet ; ten pellets of the twenty-four just penetrated the skin, and remained between the skin and the flesh.    Of the twenty-four pellets that hit the bird, twenty-one caused superficial wounds that would not have stopped its flight.

The pellet that reached the heart was the only one that would have caused the immediate collapse of the bird, though the pellet in the gullet might have led to its eventual death, and the broken wing brought it to the ground.

Average number of pellets per shot that struck the bird, six shots being fired = four.

———

No. 2.—Stationary pheasant at a height of 50 yds.    Twelve shots fired (over 3300 pellets).

RESULT.—Nine pellets lodged in the bird, or less than an average of one pellet per shot.    They inflicted slight superficial wounds, few penetrating further than the skin, and then only slightly bruising the flesh.

———

No. 3.—Stationary pheasant at a height of 60 yds.    Twelve shots fired (over 3300 pellets).

RESULT.—No pellets penetrated the skin of the bird, though

it was struck by several, as three or four dropped from its plumage when being examined.

GUN.—Pattern of 170 at a selected 30-in. circle at 40 yds., horizontal. Load: 44 grs. Schultze and $1\frac{1}{16}$ oz. No. 6, 287 to 289 pellets to the charge.[1]

Putting on one side the question of penetration, these records show the less number of pellets that are likely to strike the under-surface of a high pheasant, even though it is stationary and easy to shoot at, compared to the number that would show inside the outline of a mark the same size, when taken, as in Series VI., VII., VIII., from a selected pattern on a large target. In Series IX. twelve shots were fired at the 50- and 60-yd. heights. In Series VII. and VIII. only six shots at each height.

---

The difference, optical illusion though it may be, in the apparent size of a pheasant—as seen by the shooter—at 40 yds. perpendicular and at 40 yds. horizontal is interesting in connection with a correct aim.[2]

[1] As I wished to give as much force to the shot-pellets as possible, I previously experimented at Petitts's pads with an ounce of No. 6 and 36 grs. E.C., and then with 46 grs. of Schultze, but with very poor results both as regards pattern and penetration. I scarce expected anything else, as nothing is more certain in a game-gun than that if it is overloaded with powder, its pattern, and, as a sequence, its penetration, is inferior. If shot-pellets are driven out of a barrel with too high an initial velocity, a large proportion of them scatter and whirl away from the line of aim. It is not unusual, however, to hear of a shooter who uses an overdose of powder and an underdose of shot, in the mistaken idea that such a load will assist him to kill very high or distant birds. This theory has been over and over again proved unsound in every respect.

[2] I take the shooter as having normal long sight, and thus able to plainly see a high bird without eye-glasses. Though our eyes are lenses, and, like other lenses

In the sketches, Figs. 5, 6, 7, the apparent size of the birds is given as seen by the shooter when they are measured at the muzzle of his gun, the gun being at the shoulder and directed towards them.

The measurements were taken from dead birds slung from the kite-line, their wings, heads, and tails being extended by wires. Small callipers were attached to the muzzle of a gun, and were so arranged that they could be set to the dimensions of the birds without taking the gun from the shoulder.

By this method the perpendicular and horizontal measurements of the birds were obtained with the callipers fixed at exactly the same distance from the eye of the shooter.

An overhead object appears, if measured, much smaller than one at the same distance away on the ground. Even if we view from a distance, so as not to foreshorten his figure, a man working on the top of a high building, he looks a dwarf in comparison to what he would do if standing the same space from us on the pavement. A small and round balloon gives precisely the same effect.

It is surprising how small, to what is imagined, the apparent size of an object is if measured as the eye sees it.

A high pheasant may suggest a mark to aim at that is a couple of feet in length, though it could scarce be

may vary, yet I have found very slight difference between the apparent size at which one long-sighted person sees an object and that at which another sees it, if they measure its dimensions with callipers, in each case, of course, at the same distance from the eye. I have heard it disputed that a bird high overhead can, through an optical illusion, appear smaller to the eye than one seen horizontally, and near the ground. Though theory has been adduced to prove this to be an incorrect conclusion, yet the fact is beyond question, as anyone who, like myself, has made careful practical tests must realise.

measured between the finger and thumb without their touching each other.

No object can, however, be actually larger or smaller to our vision than we see it, though optical delusion and imagination may wrongly influence our idea of its size. This is certainly discursive, though in some degree relative to the killing of a high pheasant.

The extremely small mark offered by the 40-yd. high pheasant, as seen by the eye of the shooter, in Fig. 7,

FIG. 5.—Pheasants flying horizontally at 40 yds., 20 ft. above ground, showing their apparent size as seen by the shooter.

makes the forward allowance we should wish to give it most difficult to determine with accuracy, and this has much to do with a possible failure to kill it. On the other hand a low, though equally distant, crossing bird (Fig 5), owing to its

FIG. 6.—Pheasants flying overhead at 40 yds., showing their apparent size as seen by the shooter.

much greater apparent size, as seen by the shooter, is far easier to judge the pace of, and at the same time give a correct forward allowance to.

The orthodox way to kill a high pheasant, whether coming directly overhead, or a little to one side or the other, is to first

FIG. 7.—The upper edge of the muzzle of a double gun, and an over-head pheasant at 40 yds., showing their apparent size as seen by the shooter.

quickly realise its line of flight as indicated by its head and neck.

Then, with a more or less, as required, forward allowance, to swing the gun in the direction the bird is flying and pull trigger, if possible, without consciously checking the movement of the gun : in fact, to a slight extent, try to ' carry through,' as it is termed in golf, though you cannot really do this, as the gun must cease swinging when it is discharged.

The space at the moment of pulling trigger, between the muzzle of the gun and the head of the bird, to be the same as it was at the commencement of the swing, when the gun was, in order to gain, primarily, this space ahead of the bird, at first jerked quickly forward rather than swung forward.[1]

[1] Though it is impossible to measure feet and inches in the air in front of an overhead pheasant, still, if we could do so, here are the approximate allowances that should be made for birds flying at 40 miles an hour, or 60 ft. per second. This is an average speed for a high pheasant on a calm day, but one much increased if the wind is strong and in favour of the bird's flight. These allowances are for the centre of the shot-pattern, and include the separate one pertaining to the gun, as explained on page 7.

|  |  |  |  |  |
|---|---|---|---|---|
| At 30 yds. | . | . | . | 7 ft. |
| „ 35 „ | . | . | . | 8 „ |
| „ 40 „ | . | . | . | 9 „ |

Another system is to aim at an imaginary point in the air which the shooter supposes to be a certain fixed distance in front of an overhead or a crossing bird. Here we have trouble, as it is most difficult to shoot several feet ahead of fast-flying game and snap off a gun into space without some amount of hesitation, chiefly caused by a questioning in the mind as to distance and accuracy of aim ; and, however slight such hesitation, it means a trifling dwell on the trigger.

This slight dwell on the trigger allows the bird time to fly from its original position several feet nearer to the point ahead of it which the shooter fires his gun at, and hence, perhaps, the bird does not receive half the forward allowance necessary, and a miss behind is a frequent result.

If a shooter fires his gun at an imaginary point in the air in front of a bird crossing to one side of him, he is very apt to shoot too high or too low, unless he is able—a difficult matter—to accurately realise the inclination of its line of flight ; for when the bird has flown as far as the point where the shot-charge is designed to intercept it, it may be several feet above or below this point.

One of the very few shooters I ever knew who could successfully snap off a gun ahead of a high or a crossing pheasant, and who was also a fine shot, was the late Duke of Wellington. The Duke used to keep his gun down till his bird was just within range. He then put his gun up and fired forward of his bird in an instant, as quick as one takes a snapshot at a disappearing snipe, and at the moment the stock of the gun touched his shoulder.

I was never able to detect the least sign of swing or dwell on the trigger, and yet I have seen him kill a couple of very high pheasants in the time it would occupy an ordinary good shot to kill one of them, when swinging his gun on his bird in the usual way.

---

There is one question relative to the overhead pheasant that I should refer to, and this is the killing of the bird when it has passed behind the shooter.

It is not usual, and is seldom satisfactory, to pull trigger at a bird of this kind ; though if the shooter happens to have wounded it in front of him, he will, of course, endeavour to stop its career.

A very high bird that has flown overhead and been missed, is best left alone, as firing at it after it has passed is generally useless, and hence unsportsmanlike.

It is, as a rule, useless to do so, because the pellets of shot strike a bird flying away with about half the force they would strike the same bird when flying towards the shooter. This specially applies to a fast-driven grouse or pheasant, as the shot seldom reaches the mark before the latter is 40 yds. from the shooter, if he had to right-about-face to fire at it.

When firing at an approaching bird the shot meets it, and its pace as it flies against the pellets causes them to strike with great penetrative force.

When a bird is flying away, at a high speed, the shot has to overtake it, and, as both are travelling rapidly in the same direction, the striking-energy of the former is only about half as much as it would be if it was meeting the bird.[1]

---

[1] This does not apply to a bird rising in front, as when walking up game, as in this case it has not attained its full speed when shot at, or nearly what its pace would be if it had been driven over the shooter from a distance.

If we take the velocity of No. 6 shot and deduct from it the speed at which a fast pheasant, that has passed, might be flying, it is easy to arrive at the striking-velocity of the pellets, which, as I have said, is approximately half what it would be if the bird was approaching.

Take, for example, a football, or a punch-ball such as boxers practise with, suspended by a cord from the ceiling.

If we strike the ball with the closed fist as it swings away, the impact of the blow is as nothing compared to what it is when the ball is hit on its return swing towards us.

As the ball swings away, it may be said to represent the tail-shot at a bird, and as it swings back again, the approaching shot.

This shows how difficult it is to kill a bird from even an ordinary distance behind, that has flown fast overhead, putting on one side the fact that its vital parts are so slightly exposed to the gun.

A fast going-away pheasant generally requires to be hit with many more pellets to kill it than it would require if it were coming towards the gun and flying against the shot.

Even a tall pheasant, straight overhead—as it is not then meeting the shot—does not receive such a killing blow from the charge as it would if it were fired at, as I have advised, before it attained this position—that is, when it was a few yards to the front of the shooter, though, of course, high above ground.

If a high pheasant that has passed has, however, to be shot at, the aim, I would almost say, cannot be too low. It should be at least, to all appearance, a yard beneath the mark, or, at all events, below and clear of it, and never directly at it.   The shot-charge, as it rises, will then have a chance of intercepting the head and neck of the bird.

There is no swing here, merely a very quick aim and instant discharge of the gun.

---

If a shooter is missing overhead pheasants coming straight above him, let him swing forward of the left wings of the birds, instead of forward of their heads.[1]

If he shoots for the head and neck, the chances are he will place much of the shot-charge in the right wing.

The reason is, that it is difficult to regularly swing the muzzle of a gun in a true line with a straight overhead bird, as the left arm, towards the end of the movement, nearly always pulls the barrels to the left, or towards the bird's right wing.

By shooting for the left wing, or the one opposite to, or, over, your right shoulder, the pull of the left arm is allowed for—if such a fault is present—and you are more likely to hit the bird in the head and neck.   In the case of a left-handed sportsman the above directions will have to be reversed.

You can test the above by standing at right-angles to a straight line directly above you, such as a cornice in a room, the edge of a sky-light, or an over-hanging roof.   Then swing the muzzle of a gun along this line from a few feet in front of you back to a point over your head.   If you swing slowly, it is easy to avoid swinging off the line ; but if you swing

---

[1] It is hardly necessary to explain that the wing alluded to is the bird's proper right or left wing.

quickly, as you would have to do at a fast overhead pheasant, you will notice that near the end of your swing, or just when you would naturally pull trigger, the muzzle of the gun is usually an inch or two to the left of the line you have been following along. Further, you will see that at the finish of the swing the muzzle of the gun is sometimes slightly turned round to the left, the right barrel being higher than the left one, a fatal position in regard to correct aiming at a high bird.

———

I have alluded to two involuntary movements the shooter may easily give to his gun without being aware that he does so, which are very detrimental to accuracy of aim, especially in reference to a high overhead pheasant. One is the swinging of the muzzle of the gun off the mark to the left ; and I have explained how this divergence may be counteracted.

The other is the turning over of the barrels to the left, the right barrel being then higher than the left one, an inclination of the muzzle that may result in a bird being missed by several feet. The shooter may sometimes wonder how he managed to miss a not difficult overhead pheasant which he considered he was pretty sure to kill, and say to himself, ' Where on earth did the shot go that time ? ' In this case a slight turning over of the barrels to the left probably had much to do with his failure, though he was unaware of the cause.

The only method of correcting the muscular error that causes such a deviation of the barrels, is to hold them more tightly with the left hand than is usual. This will in no way check the swing of the gun or the movement of the left arm, and will give a rigidity to the barrels that retains them in a level position during the swing and the pulling of the trigger.

Though most shooters grasp the barrels only lightly with the left hand, I believe this is a wrong principle as regards swinging them in a level and steady line in front of a bird flying overhead.[1]

---

In the act of swinging a gun, the left hand and arm do everything, with the exception of a very slight bending back of the body from the hips, and the left hand is, therefore, the important factor to consider.

If the left arm is held too rigid, and nearly all the swing is, as a result, given by bending back the body, the tendency to pull the aim to the left of the mark, if overhead, is much increased, and the shot-charge may easily go to the left of a bird as big as a goose.

The left arm, though extended well along the barrel, should not be taut and stiff to the extent of making it as unyielding as a length of wood. The elbow must be a little bent if the arm is to be used as freely as the swing forward at an overhead bird requires.

---

The right hand, as the right arm is, of course, bent and acting as a loose hinge, should have nothing to do with directing the gun ; it merely steadies it, and pulls the trigger.

[1] If your cartridges happen to be overloaded, hold the barrels very tightly with the left hand, and you will be surprised how much the undue recoil of the gun is reduced in regard to your shoulder.

If the right hand holds the stock too firmly, it will surely check the easy swing that should be bestowed by the left hand and arm. It is the custom of many shooters to keep the forefinger of the right hand gently pressing against the first trigger during the time they are swinging the gun on a bird, and then, with an increased pressure, to release the lock when they decide to fire.

With the forefinger in this position the right hand necessarily grasps the stock with a fairly tight grip—too tight a one, as it checks the proper swing of the gun.

To avoid this, the finger should be clear of the first trigger till the moment the gun is to be discharged, when it should be quickly pressed against it from outside the guard, with the same action as when it is shifted to the other trigger, should a quick second shot be taken.

Printed in the United Kingdom
by Lightning Source UK Ltd.
134683UK00001B/170/A